RICE PUBLIC LIBRARY

KITTERY, MAINE

GREAT MYSTERIES

Alternative Healing

OPPOSING VIEWPOINTS®

Look for these and other exciting *Great Mysteries: Opposing Viewpoints* books:

GREAT MYSTERIES

Alternative Healing

OPPOSING VIEWPOINTS®

by Gail Stewart

Greenhaven Press, Inc.   P.O. Box 289009, San Diego, California 92128-9009

Library of Congress Cataloging-in-Publication Data

Stewart, Gail, 1949-
    Alternative healing : opposing viewpoints / by Gail Stewart.
        p. cm. — (Great mysteries)
    Summary: Examines the arguments for and against alternative healing methods such as psychic and natural healing, self-healing, and faith healing.
    Includes bibliographical references and index.
    ISBN 0-89908-083-9
    1. Alternative medicine—Juvenile literature. 2. Healing—Juvenile literature. [1. Alternative medicine. 2. Healing.] I. Title. II. Series: Great mysteries (Saint Paul, Minn.)
    R733.S84   1990
/615.8'52—dc20   90-3807
                                             CIP
                                              AC

To the memory of my father.

"When men and women lose the sense of mystery, life will prove to be a gray and dreary business, only with difficulty to be endured."

Harold T. Wilkins, author of Strange Mysteries of Time and Space

Contents

Introduction

This book is written for the curious—those who want to explore the mysteries that are everywhere. To be human is to be constantly surrounded by wonderment. How do birds fly? Are ghosts real? Can animals and people communicate? Was King Arthur a real person or a myth? Why did Amelia Earhart disappear? Did history really happen the way we think it did? Where did the world come from? Where is it going?

Great Mysteries: Opposing Viewpoints books are intended to offer the reader an opportunity to explore some of the many mysteries that both trouble and intrigue us. For the span of each book, we want the reader to feel that he or she is a scientist investigating the extinction of the dinosaurs, an archaelogist searching for clues to the origin of the great Egyptian pyramids, a psychic detective testing the existence of ESP.

One thing all mysteries have in common is that there is no ready answer. Often there are *many* answers but none on which even the majority of authorities agrees. *Great Mysteries: Opposing Viewpoints* books introduce the intriguing views of the experts, allowing the reader to participate in their explorations, their theories, and their disagreements as they try to explain the mysteries of our world.

But most readers won't want to stop here. These *Great Mysteries: Opposing Viewpoints* aim to stimulate the reader's curiosity. Although truth is often impossible to discover, the search is fascinating. It is up to the reader to examine the evidence, to decide whether the answer is there—or to explore further.

"Penetrating so many secrets, we cease to believe in the unknowable. But there it sits nevertheless, calmly licking its chops."

H.L. Mencken, American essayist

One

What Is Alternative Healing?

The woman's name is Blanche. She is short and slim, with a wide smile. She lives alone in an airy, comfortable apartment in New York City. Ten or fifteen times each weekday afternoon and evening, Blanche has visitors. Each person who comes to Blanche is ill. Although Blanche has no medical degree, she tries to cure them.

Some of those who visit Blanche are seriously ill with life-threatening diseases such as cancer, severe asthma, or kidney disease. Others come because of chronic back pain or headaches. Several women come to Blanche because they are having trouble becoming pregnant. A few people even bring sick dogs or cats.

Blanche does not advertise her healing services. She has found that people she has cured will tell their friends. She has all the business she can handle, although she is quick to point out that she is not doing this to get rich. She has a sliding scale for fees—whatever the patient can afford is acceptable. She does not accept money for healing pets or children.

It is difficult for Blanche to explain how she is able to heal. She uses no surgical tools or medicines. She does not use common doctor's office

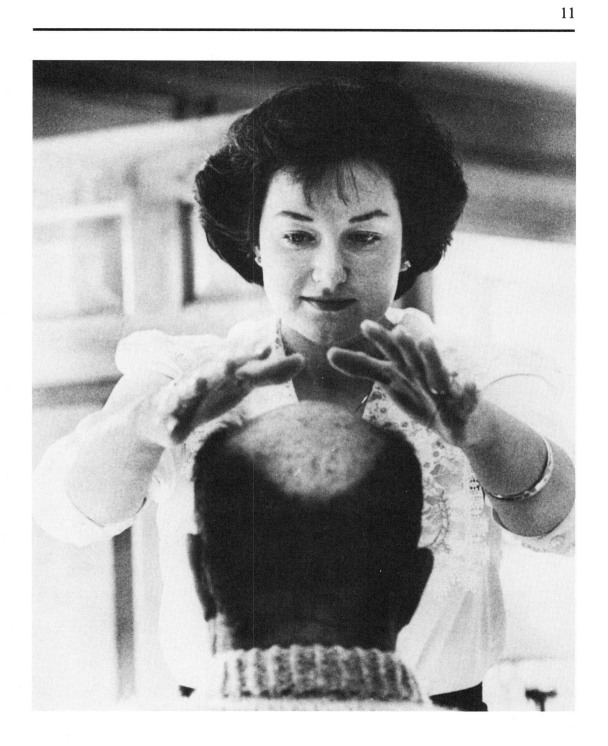

equipment, such as stethoscopes or tongue depressors. Instead, she relies on her hands. She massages, she thumps, and she prods. Sometimes she does not touch her patient's body at all—she merely passes her hands above the skin.

Blanche attributes her healing powers to six doctors in the spirit world. These doctors, explains Blanche, give her power and energy for healing that she channels into her patients. She admits she has no idea why these spirits have chosen her to do their healing. She only knows that most of her patients feel better, and many say they have been totally cured.

A Different Kind of Healing

The people who come to Blanche to be cured are seeking a different kind of healing. It involves neither medicine nor traditional doctors or therapists. It is an alternative to the kind of medical attention the majority of Americans seek when they are ill.

Instead of visiting a doctor's office, a person seeking alternative healing may see a psychic healer like Blanche. The patient may go to a

Some people seek alternative healers because they are dissatisfied with traditional doctors.

Christian faith healer, or to a Native American healer called a *shaman*. Patients may go to a person who makes concoctions of herbs, or visit a music therapist. They may decide to have their lifestyles evaluated by a *homeopath* or visit a person who specializes in something called *biofeedback*. There are more than one hundred different types of alternative healing available today.

Medical scholar Norman Oritz estimates that more than sixty million Americans have at one time or another used a healing system apart from regular medical doctors. Those people range from the poor to the very wealthy and include all cultures and races.

Why Choose Alternatives?

There are several reasons people choose alternative healing methods over regular medical care. Some feel that traditional medicine is too impersonal. Doctors are often so busy that they have little time to get to know their patients.

"I sometimes felt like my doctor didn't really have time to listen," says a 31-year-old Detroit woman suffering from abdominal pains. "He almost always arrived for appointments late, and he often seemed preoccupied—as if he were thinking about someone else's case. Was it my imagination, or did he have to check my chart to get my name right? I chose him because he was considered the leading specialist in his field. Maybe that was my mistake—everyone else had chosen him, too!"

There are also complaints about the high costs of traditional medicine. No other nation spends as much as the United States on health care. Journalist Gary Null reports that $385 billion is spent every year on traditional health care in America. That works out to approximately two thousand dollars for every man, woman, and child!

"Regular medicine is the most effective system I know for dealing with many common and serious problems."

Dr. Andrew Weil, *Health and Healing*

"Ninety percent of cases commonly seen by a physician would recover sooner or later, with more or less difficulty, provided nothing were done to interfere seriously with the efforts of nature."

Oliver Wendell Holmes, nineteenth-century physician and author

Many cultures have a long tradition of healing practices. Here, a Papago medicine man adds his skills to those of the hospital doctors.

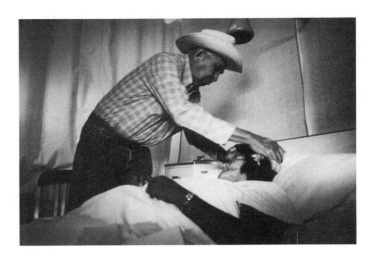

Doctors' fees and hospital costs are rising yearly. Even before a doctor knows what is making a person sick, costs can build. Blood tests, electronic scans, biopsies, X-rays, and hundreds of other diagnostic tools are extremely expensive. Once the cause for an illness is found, the pills, ointments, tonics, and salves to cure it can be costly, too.

Health insurance with steadily rising rates often covers much of the cost of traditional health care. However, millions of Americans have no health insurance—they simply cannot afford it. As a result, traditional medicine has been accused by some as biased against the poor. They say the ones who benefit from the state-of-the-art equipment and high-tech machines are those wealthy enough to pay for it.

Too Much Focus on Symptoms, Not Causes

Another reason many people turn away from traditional medicine is that they feel regular doctors focus too much on symptoms, often ignoring the causes of the disease. A traditional doctor might find a strong painkiller to help relieve a patient's tension headaches, for instance. However, the real source of the headaches—perhaps a stressful job—might be ignored. And, say critics of traditional medicine, many ailments are caused by anxiety, stress, and nervousness. Ulcers, high blood pressure, and headaches are just a few of the diseases that are brought on or worsened by stress. If the stress and anxiety are not eliminated, some argue, the disease will never be cured. The symptoms may disappear with medication, but the real cause will not be addressed.

Traditional doctors' reliance on medication is another reason some people have turned to alternative healing methods. In the last twenty years, many drugs that were once thought safe have been found extremely dangerous. Some have side effects that are, in some cases, more of a problem than the original disease!

"My three-year-old is prone to severe ear infections," says a woman from St. Paul, Minnesota. "The doctor prescribed an antibiotic to clear up the infection, but that medicine made her stomach upset. I asked about changing to a different medicine, but the doctor said no, she needed that strong dosage to kill the infection.

"Her stomachaches got so painful, he put her on a second medicine—to make her stomach feel better. That medicine made her so hyper she couldn't sleep. When the doctor suggested a third medicine to calm her down, I said 'Enough's enough!' "

A final reason some people turn away from traditional medicine is that its curing powers are limited. A man who is told he has incurable cancer or a woman who becomes paralyzed from a fall does not want to be told that doctors cannot help. Instead of accepting the fact that they will not get well, they may turn to a healing system that offers them hope.

"We have, in the United States, focused on far too narrow means of healing, the physical, the chemical—drugs and surgery. I feel that these are too limited a frame of reference."

Researcher Dr. George Araki

"The witch doctor succeeds for the same reason all the rest of us [doctors] succeed. Each patient carries his own doctor inside him."

Albert Schweitzer, twentieth-century physician and philosopher

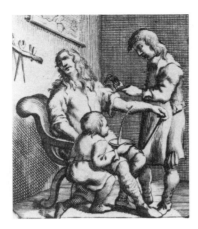

For centuries, the practice of "bleeding" a patient was important to medicine. People thought that by letting the "bad blood" out, only good, healthy blood would remain.

A Short History

It might surprise you to know that what we call "traditional medicine" has not been around for long. In fact, medicine's reliance on drugs and surgery is less than fifty years old!

The first doctors in America (not including the healers among Native American tribes) were schooled in Europe. In those days, no one was really sure what caused disease. No one had identified germs or viruses. In fact, the leading theory of the late eighteenth century was that disease was caused by "bad blood." Doctors were not certain how blood became bad, but it was thought that to rid the body of disease, the bad blood had to be removed from the body.

The years from the late 1700s to the mid 1800s have been called "The Age of Heroic Medicine." The term "heroic" refers to the energetic, aggressive role doctors took to fight disease. Few, if any, realized that the doctors' heroic actions often killed the patients.

The most common heroic measure doctors used was "bleeding" the patient. Using a sharp knife called a *lancet,* a doctor would cut into one of the patient's main arteries. After making the cut, the blood would flow freely into a bowl. (In some cases, scores of leeches were used to suck the "bad blood" from a patient.) Doctors usually

This old illustration shows English country women gathering leeches for medical use.

took a pint or more of blood at one time; the process was repeated as often as was needed.

One of the leading members of the medical community in early America was a doctor named Benjamin Rush. Besides being one of the signers of the Declaration of Independence, Rush was a firm believer in bleeding. Historians record that Rush once bled a patient eighty-five times over a six-month period!

Although to us it may appear to be a foolish idea, bleeding patients was considered the best care available. Indeed, President George Washington himself was bled by doctors—some historians now say the bleeding probably hastened his death in 1789.

President Washington had come down with a bad sore throat, and his doctor quickly decided to remove a pint of Washington's blood. The symptoms did not go away, and over the next two days three more pints were taken. Doctors now say that Washington must have been so weak and dehydrated from the bleeding that he could not fight off the infection causing the sore throat.

As the years went by, people learned that heroic medicine was not the answer. Too few people were recovering from disease, and too many were getting sicker because of the heroic measures. Many people turned away from heroic medicine. Some experimented with alternatives such as homeopathy (see chapter 5) and the use of herbs to cure disease. Many people, particularly in rural areas, stuck to a system of healing called "folk medicine." This involved a number of spells and potions that had been handed down through generations.

By the 1930s, however, many new medical discoveries had been made. Germs and viruses were identified. Researchers developed new "wonder drugs" capable of killing deadly infec-

Benjamin Rush, a prominent doctor in colonial America, was a firm believer in bleeding patients.

By the 1930s many viruses and germs were being identified as causes of disease. Scientists were finding new kinds of cures for illnesses. This picture shows a culture of penicillin, a mold with curative powers few had previously imagined.

tions. Vaccines were introduced that could keep people safe from some dangerous diseases.

Science was making surgery safer, too. Specialized new instruments and safer anesthetics helped remove many of the risks of operations. Traditional medicine had come a long way from the heroic age—in a very short time!

Questioning Alternative Medicine

Traditional medicine today is based on the idea that there is a scientific explanation for disease. The doctor's role is to diagnose the problem and then to cure it, if possible.

In many alternative healing systems, however, science is not a part of healing. Disease is often seen not as a collection of bacteria, but as an imbalance within the body. Sometimes the imbalance is due to the wrong sorts of food, or stress, or even negative thoughts.

In most alternative healing systems, the healer is only part of the cure. Sometimes the healer calls on magic to do the healing, sometimes on God, sometimes on the patients themselves.

Alternative healing methods vary greatly, and they all differ from traditional medicine. Yet healers who are not doctors claim to have cured people without drugs, without surgery, and without any of the tools of regular doctors.

The medical establishment insists that, for the most part, alternative healers are at best ineffective and at worst dangerous fakes. A pamphlet put out by the American Cancer Society, for example, criticizes alternative cancer treatments as a waste of time. "Proponents of any of these (natural healing) methods never offer sound, authentic, scientific proof of their effectiveness. Their records, in the rare instances they have records, are questionable. Other scientists cannot confirm their claims. Their methods remain: UNPROVEN." Other literature warns those with cancer of the danger of "wasting valuable time by trying unproven methods."

Many alternative healers do not disagree that their systems are unscientific. Blanche, the healer mentioned at the beginning of this book, admits she has no idea why her patients get better—but they do. Other healers give the credit to the patient's faith in God or to magical forces at work within the patient's body. Still other healing systems credit a specialized set of foods or vitamins.

This book will explore some alternative healing systems. It will focus on a number of puzzling questions: What exactly does a healer do that a doctor does not? Is it really possible for someone with an "incurable" disease to walk away from a healer without any trace of the disease? Is there any proof that alternative healing works?

Two

Can Faith Heal?

Many people turn to faith healers as an alternative to traditional medicine. By far, the majority of faith healers in this country are Christians, although many of the world's religions teach that by praying to a god, people can rid themselves of disease.

The Roots of Faith Healing

The first Christian faith healer was Jesus. The Bible contains many examples of Jesus healing the sick, enabling the blind to see, and even raising the dead. Christians believe that Jesus could do these things because he was the Son of God and possessed powers ordinary people did not have.

However, many Christians believe that the Bible recognizes that others may have the ability to do the kind of healing Jesus did. The New Testament contains a section widely quoted by modern faith healers. I Corinthians 12:8-10 lists nine talents, or "gifts" that God has given to people. Healing the sick and performing miracles are two of these gifts, and they are the basis of faith healers' claims.

In the early centuries of Christianity, people believed they could be cured in ways other than visiting a healer. The Catholic Church taught that the physical remains of certain holy people had

Opposite: Many people turn to faith healers when they are sick.

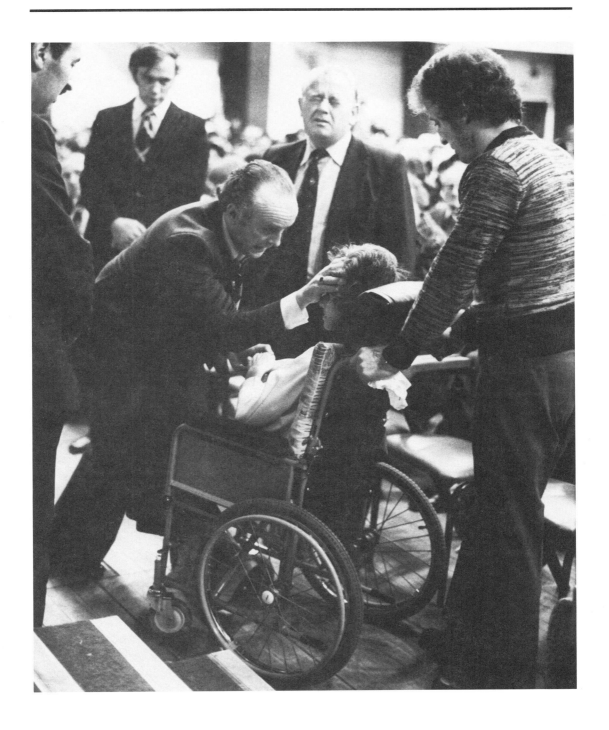

The Christian tradition of faith healing started with Jesus. But faith healers have probably existed for as many eons as religion has.

healing powers. Churches had collections of such relics.

One church claimed to have a jar containing milk from Jesus' mother Mary; another had an assortment of bones from the three wise kings who visited the baby Jesus. One church prized its collection of crusts of bread and fish bones left over from Jesus' feeding of the five thousand. Another church claimed it had an entire skeleton of one of Christ's disciples; still another had a single hair from Jesus' beard.

People believed that by touching one of these sacred relics, a sick person could become well.

And because they believed, too, that disease was the result of evil spirits or demons, it seemed correct that the power of God could defeat the powers of evil and heal them.

The Royal Touch

Religious faith healing changed greatly in the next several centuries. Many kings who ruled Europe in the fourteenth and fifteenth centuries believed that their power to rule was granted by *divine right*. In other words, they ruled because God had ordered it so. This notion changed the whole idea of why people became kings. It was not simply a matter of one person having more power than anyone else. Kings began to be viewed as "chosen" people—perhaps because of their talents or wisdom.

Since their political power came from God, many of these kings decided that they might also have other divine gifts. Healing was one of these.

In 1307, King Philip of France announced that he was blessed with a "royal touch." Any of his subjects who were suffering from an illness could come to him and be cured simply by his touch. Other royalty in Europe followed Philip's example and claimed the royal touch, too. According to legend, some people were cured of disease. No one knows, of course, if the "cures" were actual or not. However, some historians have speculated that some of Philip's subjects falsely claimed that they were cured in order to flatter the king and win his favor.

The belief in miraculous royal touch faded as people learned more about the human body. As early scientists began to have some understanding of disease and the way the human body works, the miraculous healings of the kings and religious leaders seemed less believable.

"See! Hear! Actual miracles happening before your eyes. Cancer, tumors, goiters disappear. Crutches, braces, wheelchairs, stretchers discarded."

1957 television ad for faith healer A. A. Allen

"I have seen no miracles. In fact, I've had to run diabetics to the hospital when they've stopped taking their insulin, believing they had been cured in Miracle Valley."

Kenneth A. Dregseth, physician

During the Middle Ages in Europe, people thought kings had the divine power to heal. This nineteenth-century illustration shows King Charles II of England healing one of his subjects.

A Miraculous Healing Place?

Faith healing also occurs in holy places, some people believe. The most famous of these holy places is a little town called Lourdes, in the south of France. Throughout the past century, Lourdes was known as a place many seriously ill people visited to be cured.

In 1858 a young peasant girl named Bernadette Soubirous told people that she had been visited by the Virgin Mary in Lourdes, France. Many church officials believed her story, and several years later a church and shrine were built on the site. There is a spring at Lourdes, too, and many people began bathing in the icy water, thinking that it had miraculous healing powers.

Many thousands of people claimed they were cured of a wide range of diseases—from arthritis to blindness, from asthma to cancer. Officials of the Catholic Church set up a committee whose job it was to investigate such claims. Was the spring at Lourdes really a source of miraculous cures? The Church wanted to be very careful about such an astounding idea.

The committee made strict rules about what would be considered a true healing at Lourdes. The individual had to have well-documented proof of a disease before visiting the shrine and again after a cure took place. Blood tests, X-rays, or some other medical proof had to be provided. Such documentation would eliminate those who might simply "feel better" after visiting Lourdes but who were not rid of disease.

Since it became a shrine in 1876, Lourdes has changed drastically. Tourism is the town's chief source of income. Hundreds of souvenir stands sell tiny plastic vials of spring water and pictures of the Virgin Mary. More than four hundred hotels have been built to accommodate the five million people who visit Lourdes each year.

Of the millions of cures claimed since the shrine opened, only sixty-four have been accepted by Church officials as truly miraculous. The most famous of these is the cure of a young Italian man named Vittorio Micheli.

Micheli was diagnosed by doctors as having a cancerous growth on his hip. The cancer had grown between his pelvis and hip bone, separating the two, and causing Micheli great pain. Because the disease had advanced so far, doctors told Micheli there was nothing they could do to cure him. His doctors estimated that he had only a few weeks to live. They did put a heavy plaster cast around the separated bones, however, so that no further separation could take place.

Micheli, like many others in his apparently hopeless situation, decided to try for a miracle cure at Lourdes. On May 24, 1963, weak and unable to walk, he dragged himself to the edge of the spring and plunged into the water. Immediately he felt better. He told officials later that he ex-

In 1858 in Lourdes, France, a devout girl named Bernadette Soubirous, saw a vision of the Virgin Mary. The cove where Bernadette was visited by the Virgin is still believed by many to be a place of divine healing.

perienced a feeling of warmth and happiness. He felt energized and hungry (sensations he had not felt for some time) and pronounced himself cured. In less than a month, Micheli was able to walk, and doctors removed his cast.

X-rays taken since Micheli's visit to Lourdes show that the large cancerous growth is no longer there. His pelvis and hip bone have grown back together, and there is no evidence of disease. His doctors were astounded, calling the cure "remarkable" and "of a type unknown in the annals of world medicine."

Doubting Scientists

Not all medical experts are convinced that Lourdes is a source of faith healing. Some feel that visitors to Lourdes want so desperately to be cured that they wrongly convince themselves that they feel better. Dr. Daniel Stern, a cancer specialist from New York City, has seen one of his patients experience such a "cure."

"It is very common for a person to feel better after an emotional experience," states Dr. Stern. "After a particularly exciting moment, such as dipping in the water at Lourdes, or going onstage at a faith healing meeting, a person's adrenalin is on 'high.' Pain and discomfort are forgotten, at least for the moment. But after an hour, or a day, or a week, the pain comes back. The disease, of course, was never really gone in the first place."

But what about cases that are well-documented, such as Micheli's? Doctors are not as sure. Some have suggested that the cancer was incorrectly diagnosed, or that the X-rays were not properly interpreted. Too, it is important to understand that there have been instances of unexplained, spontaneous cures of cancer and other life-threatening diseases without the help of a miraculous place. In such cases, the tumor or

"What you see at these services is not fortunetelling. What you see at these services is not magic tricks. What you see at these services is 'HSP': Holy Spirit Power!"

Faith healer W.V. Grant

"[Faith healers] appear to be pious and innocent, but have perpetrated a vicious, callous, and highly profitable scam on their flocks, bringing grief, economic loss, and severe health risks to their victims."

James Randi, *The Faith Healers*

Opposite: The shrine at Lourdes is one of many holy places in the world where pilgrims go to be healed.

These are a few of the many millions of pilgrims who visit Lourdes each year and bathe in its waters, hoping for a cure.

growth simply shrinks and eventually disappears. This has occurred without surgery, medicine, or radiation therapy. Although such cures are quite rare, they have happened, and doctors offer no real explanation for them. Perhaps, say some medical authorities, the Micheli case was one of these unusual cases.

Zion—The Healing City

In the early twentieth century, another kind of faith healing became popular. People who called themselves faith healers claimed that they had the gift of miracles and healing talked about in the Bible. They urged people with health problems to come to them and be cured.

The first well-known faith healer in America was John Dowie. He believed that doctors and medicine were dangerous and that they caused more health problems than they cured. They were, according to Dowie, "the foes of Christ the Healer," for they encouraged people to trust in other human beings instead of God for health.

Dowie felt that Christ could heal most effectively through a human faith healer such as Dowie himself. He established a city based on this belief—Zion, Illinois—halfway between Milwaukee and Chicago. In the early 1900s, Zion's population of believers grew to over ten thousand.

Tent Meetings

Most of the early faith healers did not establish permanent headquarters like Dowie did. They chose instead to travel from town to town, preaching and healing in various churches along the way. Often, their healing ceremonies were so popular that a small village church would scarcely be large enough to hold the crowds. In these cases, large tents would be set up, and the healing services were held there.

Just as many visitors to the shrine at Lourdes said they had been healed, many who came forward at these tent meetings claimed that the faith healers had cured them. The process varied little between healers. There would be lots of singing and clapping, and the healer would begin to talk.

Healers were always very accomplished speakers and were able to command the interest and enthusiasm of the crowds. The healer would remind the audience that disease is the work of evil, or the devil. He or she would remind them, too, that the only way to fight the devil is with the healing of Jesus. All that was needed for a cure, according to the healer, was a strong and unwavering faith in Jesus' healing power.

Midway through the healing session, the healer would invite the sick and handicapped to come forward. As they approached the platform—either on foot, or with the use of crutches, canes, or wheelchairs—the healer and the audience would applaud or shout words of encouragement to them.

Once they were in the front of the church or

John Dowie, America's first famous faith healer, founded a city called Zion for his followers.

Oral Roberts is a modern faith healer. This picture, taken in 1958, shows him healing a young boy at a prayer and healing service in England.

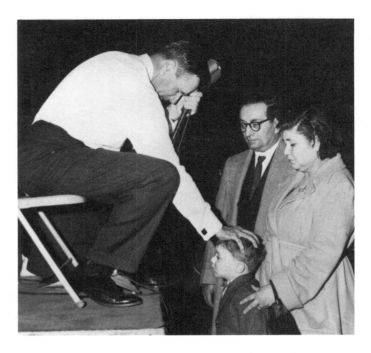

tent, the participants would be asked a few questions: What was the nature of their disease? Did they accept Jesus as the true healer in their lives?

One healer might put his hands on the head of the person and pray. Another might snap her fingers or cry out over the person's head. Some healers would circle each participant, mumbling soft prayers. Still others would actually strike each person on the shoulder, knocking them to the ground. This method was very dramatic, for the participants appeared to be unconscious on the ground for several minutes. The healer would tell the audience that they had been "smitten by the healing of the Holy Spirit."

Although no statistics exist about the number of people cured of pain or disease at these tent meetings, the faith healers were quite popular. When word came to a town that a healer would be arriving, crowds from all over the county would gather. As one historian writes, "It seemed that everyone had a mother, a son, a grandfather, a cousin—someone who'd been saved by a visiting healer. Stories abounded—a child dying of tuberculosis who had been made well; a blind woman who could now see; a man with a bad leg who no longer needed crutches."

The Modern Faith Healer

The faith healer of today has come a long way from the tent meetings of several decades ago. Although the actual healing ceremonies are the same, the ways people can participate are very different. Tens of millions of people listen to healers on the radio or watch them on television. Several of the most popular faith healers have their own weekly shows. Healers also make highly publicized public appearances. It is not uncommon for a faith healer to draw fifty thousand people to a single "healing explosion," as these large events are sometimes called!

Names such as Pat Robertson, Rex Humbard, Jim Bakker, and Oral Roberts have become internationally famous because of such media coverage. Hundreds of thousands of people have come up to faith healers such as these, begging to be healed. Many claim that their diseases and pain have disappeared because of faith healers.

Nadine Belker is an 83-year-old North Carolina woman. She came forward in a healing explosion in 1985. Five years later she said, "I had arthritis real bad in my fingers. I had trouble writing checks or even using the can opener. I heard a healer on the radio say that no one needs to suffer like that, and it was just a matter of believing and coming forward. I visited a [healing] show and came forward like they said. My pain is gone now."

Tarell Reed agrees. He had chronic back pain

These people participated in a huge healing service in New Orleans's Superdome in 1988.

Many faith healers have their own television programs. During their services, they not only try to heal people in their immediate audience, but they claim to heal television watchers as well.

until he attended an Oral Roberts healing event in 1982. "I used to bite on my lip because of the pain in my back. I didn't want to cry out," says Reed. "My nephew pushed me up the aisle in a wheelchair. But I was healed, and [Roberts] said, 'Get up from that old chair,' and I did. I don't need the blasted thing at all. Jesus took my pain away."

Miracles or Melodrama?

Many people doubt that the faith healers are really healing. Instead, they claim that the healing event is often "staged" to look as though people are being miraculously healed. One critic has called such healing events "more melodrama than miracles."

Writer Joe Barnhart visited a healing service performed by the famous W. V. Grant. Barnhart observed that a great number of the "sick" who came forward in wheelchairs to be cured had not arrived in those wheelchairs. Grant's staff had supplied the chairs to people who were willing to come forward to be healed. As these people were touched by Grant, they stood up from their chairs at his urging. While the audience applauded, Grant's "patients" pushed their empty wheelchairs back up the aisle. According to Barnhart, the audience wrongly assumed that these people had been miraculously allowed to walk when they had not even needed the wheelchairs in the first place!

Surgeon William Nolen also visited a miracle healing service and was highly critical. Allowed to work as an usher at a Kathryn Kuhlman healing event, Nolen noticed Kuhlman's staff urging some people with minor ailments to come forward in wheelchairs or even on stretchers. This audience, too, was given the false impression that miraculous "healing" had given them the power to walk on their own.

Nolen did see some people walk away from Kathryn Kuhlman more energetically than when they first approached her. Some had been in obvious pain before being healed, and their pain appeared to be gone, or at least lessened. Nolen believed, however, that the emotional "high" the people felt had deadened their pain. The singing, stamping and clapping of the audience, as well as the people's own expectations of being healed actually convinced them that the healing was genuine. Unfortunately, such emotional highs do not permanently rid the body of pain. It usually returns within hours of the emotional experience.

A Cruel Theology?

Another criticism of faith healers comes not from doctors but from other religious leaders. They worry that faith healers are creating an atmosphere in which disease is seen as a punishment for not believing in God. Some have called this the "gospel of health and wealth." Simply put, it means that people are sick only because they have not put their trust in God. The moment they declare their undying trust, they can be cured. On the other hand, those who continue to be sick

This woman is attempting to heal the man in the wheelchair. Even the most widely publicized healers do not claim to heal everyone who comes to them, but they try to offer some hope and relief from discomfort.

In the 1980s, a series of scandals plagued famous faith healers. This couple, Tammy Faye and Jim Bakker, were accused of financial and sexual misbehavior. Some people believe all "faith healers" are frauds.

after visiting a faith healer are guilty of not believing strongly enough.

Minneapolis minister Russell Friend-Jones grew up in a small West Virginia town. He saw firsthand how devastated someone can be when they are *not* healed.

"My grandmother was very ill with a degenerative bone disease. She couldn't walk without the aid of crutches. The doctors had given her very little hope, and she was in a great deal of pain. When the healer came to our town, she had my grandfather take her to the service.

"When it came time to be healed, she painfully made her way to the front of the meeting. After the clapping and the singing, the healer prayed over her. He told her to throw down her crutches. He said that she was healed, and she didn't need them any more.

"She was a devout Baptist. She believed she'd been healed and tried to walk without them. She tried more than once, but she couldn't do it. He ended up literally running her out of the healing meeting. He was angry, and told her that she

Part of nearly all healing services is the call from the minister for financial help. Some people say that the "healers" are healing their own pocketbooks and not their petitioners. Others say that money is necessary for the ministries to do their work and is unrelated to the gift of healing.

would never get well because she just wasn't a believer."

Hoax or Healing?

Appeals for donations are a key part of every healing service. This, coupled with the fact that healers are not required to report such earnings to the Internal Revenue Service, makes many people suspicious. They have pointed to the lavish lifestyles of many faith healers. Scandals in the late 1980s surrounding the financial and personal activities of healers like Jimmy Swaggart and Jim Bakker have fueled some of this criticism.

Other criticism is leveled by people like William Nolen who want to see real proof of cure—not a mere disappearance of symptoms. If faith can heal, askes Nolen, why can the faith healers not help a new leg grow where one has been amputated, or help a child whose face is distorted because of a birth defect?

Although such questions have not been answered, faith healers continue to attract millions of people who believe that they can be cured. To them, and to the many thousands who say they have already been cured by faith healers, it makes no difference whether the healers' claims can be proven or not. To them it is a matter of belief, not science.

"Healers can't cure organic diseases. Physicians can."

Dr. William A. Nolen, *Healing*

"During the five weeks of a doctors' strike in Los Angeles in 1976, the weekly death rate in hospitals dropped below normal for that time of year. Analysts attributed the drop to unnecessary operations that were not performed."

Dr. Andrew Weil, *Health and Healing*

Three

Do Self-Healing Methods Work?

Some alternatives to traditional medicine work without healers. They rely on the body's supposed ability to heal itself. These self-healing methods are based on the notion that the human body contains hundreds, perhaps thousands, of substances that can cure diseases ranging from a sore throat to cancer. Many of these self-healing abilities are very difficult to develop at first. However, many advocates of self-healing insist that with training, anyone can tune in to the subtle healing powers of his or her body.

Iridology

Traditional doctors use many methods to *diagnose,* or discover, a disease or other condition. To find whether a person has an infection, a technician views a drop of blood under a microscope. A small piece of cotton dabbed on a person's tongue can be used to diagnose strep throat. To discover the presence of diabetes, laboratory technicians need a small amount of a patient's urine.

Sometimes the diagnostic procedures are more involved. Often tissue samples are cut from a tumor or organ and examined closely. This type

Opposite: Some people look within themselves for the power to heal. They believe people have tremendous inner resources that can triumph over illness.

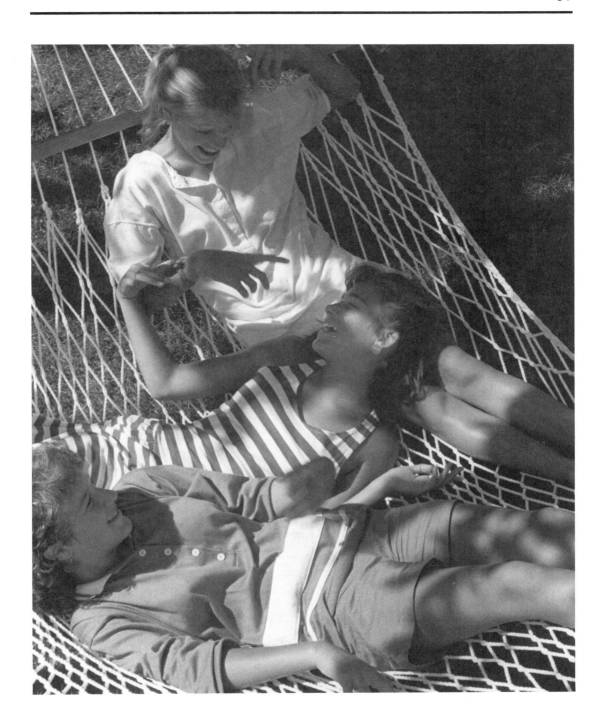

Iridologists believe that accurate medical diagnoses can be made without "invading" the body with blood tests, biopsies, CAT scans, and so forth. All the clues to the body's state of health, they say, are found in the iris of the eye.

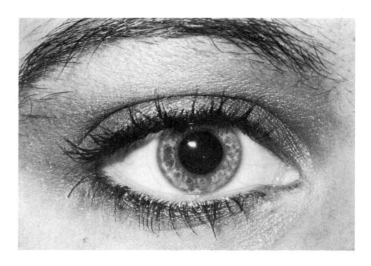

of diagnosis is called a *biopsy*. Many forms of cancer are diagnosed in this way.

Iridology is a different sort of diagnostic tool. It is based on the belief that the colored part, or *iris,* of a person's eye changes when he or she is ill. Iridologists believe that by looking at what part of the iris changes, and the way in which the color is different, they can detect the presence of disease.

From an Owl's Broken Leg

Iridology is not a new method. It was begun in the mid-nineteenth century by a Hungarian doctor named Ignatz von Peczely. As a child, von Peczely owned a pet owl. One day, he was careless about the handling of the bird and broke the owl's leg.

Von Peczely noticed immediately that there was a change in the owl's irises. A small, dark bar appeared in the colored center of the owl's eyes and remained there until the leg had healed. Fascinated by what had happened, von Peczely took notice of other animals (including human beings) who were suffering from injuries. He was curious about whether all eyes change during injury, or whether the change in his owl's eyes was merely a coincidence.

Von Peczely found enough evidence to support his theory—that the iris is a good indicator of injury to other parts of the body. Not only did the iris show changes during injury, according to von Peczely's research, it also indicated the presence of disease. Kidney disease, heart murmers, pneumonia—all seemed to von Peczely to show up in the irises of his patients. Throughout his life, he continued to do research on this new diagnostic method.

What Iridologists Believe

In the one hundred years since von Peczely introduced his iridology theories to the world, others have added to his research. Today there are over ten thousand iridologists in Europe, and about one thousand in the United States. The leading U.S. advocate of iridology is Bernard Jensen.

This chart, based on the one developed by Dr. Bernard Jensen, shows where to look in the iris to check on the state of health of various parts of the body.

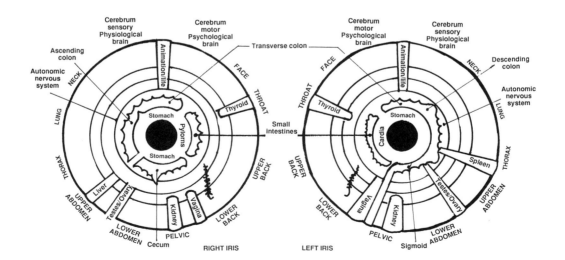

Jensen has published several books in which he expands many of von Peczely's early theories. According to Jensen's research, the iris is part of a network of nerves that are everywhere in the body. Iridologists believe that complex messages from this network are sent to the iris. These messages may be sent because of disease, injury, or stress to a particular organ. The messages show up on the iris by way of small variations in texture and color.

A person trained in iridology can look at a patient's iris and compare it with charts that have been compiled over the years. These charts show two large circles (irises), which have been divided and subdivided by lines. Within the lines, iridologists have written in parts of the body, such as liver, lungs, legs, and so on.

The iridologist's job is to compare a patient's irises with the chart. If, for example, a patient's right iris is cloudy in one tiny area, it might indicate a bad heart, a thyroid condition, or poor digestion.

Iridologists are proud of their diagnostic method. They refer to it as a *noninvasive* diagnostic tool, which means that no harm is done to the body. Traditional medicine's means of diagnosis involve needles, surgery, or X-rays, but iridology is done merely by trained observation.

Iridology Under Attack

Traditional medicine is based on the scientific method. Once a theory or idea is proposed, scientists attempt to prove that theory through controlled tests and experiments. If a theory is valid, it can be demonstrated by such tests. Its success is not left to chance; on the contrary, if it is valid, it can be proven again and again.

Iridology is not recognized as a legitimate diagnostic tool by traditional doctors. According to many doctors, iridology has not been proven in a scientific manner. The explanations of the workings of the nerve network—the heart of iridology—are not easily proven, and so far few in the medical profession agree with the idea.

No one disputes that the nerves of the body are interconnected—that much has been known for many years. But many doctors wonder how the iris, of all places in the body, is the key. How is it that the iris monitors the body's ailments?

Family physician Paul Reisser disagrees that the iris's connection to the rest of the body gives it special diagnostic powers. "Merely being connected to the [nerve] system does not prove that all of the body can be monitored," states Reisser. "My telephone is connected to a massive communications network, but it does not send me messages about the equipment or conversations of everyone in America."

The absence of reliable test results makes traditional doctors suspect iridology, too. Although iridologists claim to have done many tests, only one has been monitored by traditional doctors. That particular test, conducted at the University of California at San Diego, did not turn out well for the iridologists.

In this study, scientists wanted to learn how accurate iridolists were at spotting people who

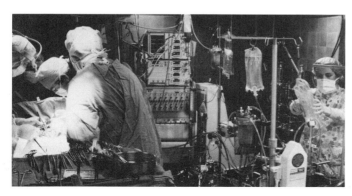

Medical doctors fear that people who believe in alternative medical methods such as iridology will fail to get more accurate, traditional medical tests. In some cases, doctors say, this could prevent proper treatment and lead to further illness or even death.

"Iridology is based on scientific observation. It is the kind of science that cannot be related through scientific tests, for it does not provide clinical information."

Iridology proponent Bernard Jensen

"Iridology's basic premise is highly suspect, and its performance has not earned a passing grade using ordinary methods of scientific investigation."

Paul Reisser, co-author of *New Age Medicine*

were seriously ill. Iridologists, including Bernard Jensen, were shown color photographs of irises of 143 subjects. Of these, 48 had severe kidney disease. The results showed that the iridologists' record for detecting kidney disease was the same as chance. In other words, by pulling names out of a hat, anyone could do as good a job spotting the seriously ill patients.

Jensen and the other iridologists who participated in the study feel that the test was unfair. They maintain that their diagnoses were accurate, that the photographs they chose as the ones with kidney disease were indeed ill. Even though those patients had not yet been stricken with kidney disease, the iridologists insisted, their irises showed that they soon would be.

Mind Cures

Dr. Franz Inglefinger, a respected medical doctor, stated that 85 percent of all people who go to doctors are suffering from "self-limiting disorders." By that Inglefinger meant that the problems did not require outside help. The ailments could, he felt, be healed by the body itself.

Advocates of self-healing believe Inglefinger's estimates are low. They feel that almost every physical problem—from AIDS and cancer to arthritis and high blood pressure—can be healed by the body itself. They believe, too, that self-healing will be the medicine of the future. They claim that the medical community has already begun to take a serious look at some of their ideas.

The Strange Case of Norman Cousins

One of these self-healing methods was developed out of desperation by a man named Norman Cousins. In 1964 Cousins began feeling ill and feverish. The symptoms progressed, making it impossible for him to continue his work as editor of *The Saturday Review.* At his doctor's urging, Cousins was admitted to a hospital for tests.

After a long series of diagnostic tests, doctors found that Cousins was suffering from a deadly disease that attacks the connective tissues of the body. Cousins felt a great deal of pain when he moved his joints—his elbows, ankles, knees, and especially his fingers. He was in so much pain, in fact, that he was unable to sleep at all.

Because the disease had progressed so rapidly in such a short time, the doctors held out little hope. They told Cousins that his disease was terminal—that is, there was little or no hope that he would recover.

Cousins had recently read a book about the negative effects of stress and worry. According to that book, such emotions made the body have to work even harder to get well. Cousins wondered if the opposite could be true. If negative emotions hindered the healing process, could it be possible that positive emotions could speed the healing process?

Realizing that he had very little to lose by trying, Cousins decided to fight back against the disease that threatened his life. He resolved that he would change his medical treatment. To start with, there would be no more hospital. He moved himself into a nearby hotel and hired a nurse. The peace and quiet, along with less clinical surroundings, seemed to him more soothing.

Then he took himself off all medications prescribed by his doctors. The only pill he took each day was a large dose of vitamin C. Last, Cousins believed that one of the most powerful of the positive emotions was humor. He obtained a supply of old movies, especially slapstick comedies. He sought out the funniest "Candid

When writer Norman Cousins was told he had an incurable disease, he determined to fight it himself. He quit traditional medical treatment and cured himself with a stress-free, positive attitude.

Norman Cousins and others believe humor is one of the keys to good health.

Camera'' episodes and had piles of funny magazines and books brought to his room.

Cousins found immediate results from his homemade ''laugh therapy.'' He learned quickly that after about ten minutes of laughing at a funny story or movie, he could fall asleep for nearly two hours—something he had been unable to do because of the intense pain.

Encouraged by this progress, he kept on over several months. Little by little, the pain in his joints subsided. Doctors repeated earlier laboratory tests and confirmed that he was, indeed, recovering. After many months Cousins was up and back at work—living proof that all terminal illnesses do not have unhappy endings.

''Spontaneous Recovery''

Norman Cousins' case was remarkable, but

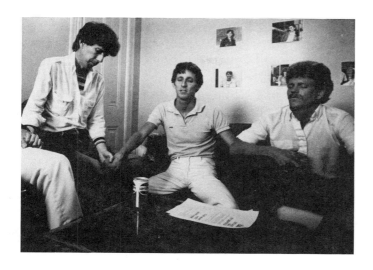

In the left picture, the man on the right has AIDS, an incurable disease. Here, he and friends try positive thinking methods to help him become well. Right: Can depression and stress prevent a cure?

for many scientists it was no proof that humor can cure disease. Although doctors documented that he had a deadly disease from which he was given almost no chance of recovery, there is no way of proving that it was the laughter that helped.

Medical doctors have a name for the rare case of a terminal patient being completely cured— *spontaneous recovery.* It means simply that some unknown factor or factors caused the disease to disappear on its own. There is no explanation for a spontaneous recovery.

Because only Cousins tried his method of healing and the method was not done under scientific conditions, it is difficult for the medical community to test it. However, other instances of a connection between positive attitudes and the body's ability to fight disease are being documented scientifically.

PNI

One of the newest branches of scientific research is called *psychoneuroimmunology,* or

PNI for short. Scientists involved in PNI are trying to prove what Norman Cousins and others have proposed—that positive attitudes can help the body heal itself.

Studies in PNI have shown that there is a connection between the mind and the body's immune system, which safeguards against disease. Disease-fighting cells are produced in the spleen and deep within the bone marrow. Researchers are suggesting that negative emotions, such as fear, stress, and rage, tend to block production of these cells. On the other hand, they think that positive emotions, such as humor, love, and forgiveness, tend to increase the disease-fighting cells.

One study done at Beth Israel Hospital in Boston seems to support this idea. Researchers there did personality assessments of a large group of college students. They were rated either as "good copers" or "bad copers." Which category a student fell into depended on his or her outlook. Was the student able to handle stress, or was it likely to throw him or her into depression?

The students, thus categorized, were given

Even many traditional doctors believe a patient's attitude can mean the difference between sickness and health. But doctors believe a good attitude has to work *with* medical treatment, not instead of it.

Friendship and emotional support help many people cope with illness.

blood tests to examine the level of disease-fighting cells in their bodies. The results showed that the bad copers had fewer of the cells than the good copers had. In other words, those with a more positive outlook tended to have a stronger immune system to fight infection and disease.

Suspicious Doctors

Even though early research in PNI suggests that positive emotions promote healing, the idea is far from proven. Many medical doctors are, in fact, suspicious of alternative healing methods that are based on "good feelings." And when advocates of such healing methods claim that they work on even serious diseases such as cancer or AIDS, many doctors strongly disagree.

One such method, developed by O. Carl Simonton, claimed that cancer patients could cure their own disease by concentrating on it. Strong mental concentration could, according to Simonton, give the immune system an added boost, enabling it to cure itself.

Not so, according to cancer specialist Wallace Sampson. He challenged Simonton to offer hard, scientific facts proving his claims. Sampson is confident that no such proof can be made. "It is highly unlikely that trying to boost the immune system through vague, hypothesized mechanisms starting with the mind would be successful," insists Sampson.

Some in the medical community have expressed concern over the mind-disease connection. Although there is admittedly some early evidence indicating that there could be a connection, they say that it could be a dangerous idea. For one thing, patients may decide to forego medical treatment. They may instead choose to use humor, as Norman Cousins did, or concentration, as Simonton suggests. For a patient with a disease like cancer, abandoning medical treatment could be fatal, say doctors. Postponing surgery or chemotherapy while trying a self-healing method might waste precious time.

Another worry of the medical community is that self-healing can put too heavy a load of responsibility on the patient. If a woman with cancer is not successful in curing herself, or even in managing her pain through self-healing, will she feel guilty, as if it were her fault? Or worse yet, will she feel that negative emotions caused her disease in the first place? Such unfounded guilt, say doctors, is more than any sick person should have to bear.

Biofeedback

One form of self-healing has limited support from at least some traditional doctors. This method is called *biofeedback*. The idea behind biofeedback is that people can learn to control certain functions of their bodies that were once believed uncontrollable.

Some bodily functions are easily controlled, such as moving our arms or wiggling a finger. We can consciously decide to make muscles move and

"In five years there will be biofeedback centers all over the country, in which people can learn all manner of mind and body functions."

Dr. Barbara Brown, biofeedback researcher

"Biofeedback researchers have published thousands of reports on their findings. Even so, hard, provable facts about biofeedback's effectiveness are difficult to come by."

Ann Weiss, *Biofeedback*

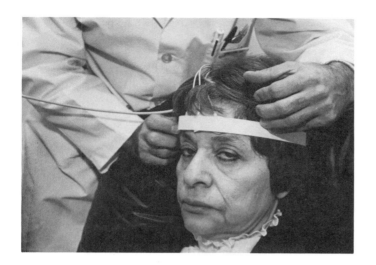

Biofeedback techniques allow people to learn how to control certain functions of their bodies that were once thought to be uncontrollable. A person is trained in biofeedback techniques with equipment such as this woman is using. Later, when the techniques are learned, no equipment is necessary.

they move. These are called *voluntary functions.* Other bodily functions are normally out of our control. These are called *involuntary functions,* and they include pulse, skin temperature, and brain waves. By using special machines, and with the careful instruction of technicians, some people have learned to control some of these involuntary functions.

One of the most common uses of biofeedback is to relieve severe headaches. Doctors know that there are different kinds of headaches. Some are caused by a tightening of the little muscles in the neck and face. Others, called *migraines,* are caused by spasms of blood vessels in the head.

Biofeedback technicians teach patients how to relax the involuntary neck and facial muscles, and in the case of migraines, the blood vessels in their heads. The teaching is accomplished by hooking the patient up to an ultra-sensitive machine. The machine has electronic monitors that can sense when a particular muscle or set of blood vessels is tight.

In a dark room, the patient tries to relax, concentrating on relaxing the tight muscles. Each

This boy is using biofeedback techniques in order to learn how to relax.

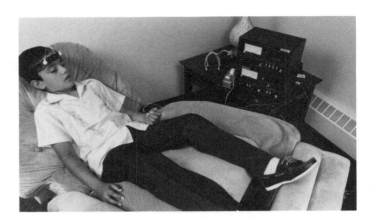

time the muscles relax, the machine clicks. The biofeedback technician explains to the patient that the idea is to get as many clicks as possible. Even though the patient is not actually aware of *how* the muscles are being relaxed, she or he knows that a certain feeling can produce a click. Over a period of time—minutes or hours, depending on the patient—the patient will be able to "teach" his or her body how to relax and produce the clicking noises on the monitor.

By controlling tiny muscles or blood vessels, the patient can avoid standard medical care. No drugs are involved, and because there is no reliance on doctors, there is no expense once the technique is learned. Many people who have mastered biofeedback techniques say that when they feel muscles tightening they can relax them before a headache starts.

Just the Beginning

In addition to healing themselves of headaches, biofeedback patients have learned to control their blood pressure. Some have learned to control delicate facial muscles after suffering a stroke. With biofeedback, they have "taught" their bodies how to blink both eyes at the same time and how to smile.

Advocates of biofeedback are enthusiastic about their healing method. Some of them feel that there are new, untried biofeedback methods that may help patients prevent ulcers or heart attacks. Others think that in the future biofeedback techniques can be used to shrink cancerous tumors. If such "automatic" functions as heartbeat and the size of blood vessels can be controlled, they say, why not things such as cell growth?

Yet some are critical of the claims of biofeedback enthusiasts. In fact, many of these critics are biofeedback researchers themselves! Some worry that the successes of biofeedback may be due, not to the healing method, but to the positive feelings patients have toward the method.

In her book *Biofeedback: Fact or Fad?,* Ann E. Weiss points out that about 75 percent of illnesses are caused by worry and stress. When that worry is lessened—in the case of biofeedback, by a supportive technician and relaxing surroundings—the symptoms often disappear. Some critics claim that overenthusiastic biofeedback researchers have been mistakenly taking credit for cures. In fact, they say, the patients were cured by relaxing and relieving their stress and anxiety.

Critics of biofeedback also worry that the research has been scant. It is difficult, perhaps impossible, to prove what caused a headache to disappear. No scientific laboratory experiments have yet been devised that can pinpoint the cause of a cure. Patients may say that biofeedback makes them "feel better," but that is hardly scientific proof.

When more research is done on larger groups of people, proponents of biofeedback may be better able to back up their impressive claims and convince those in doubt.

Four

Can Disease Be Healed by Psychic Power?

While there is some scientific evidence to support some of the self-healing methods, there is another type of healing that is not at all concerned with the world of science. *Psychic healing,* a term which covers dozens of varieties of healing, cannot be explained by controlled laboratory studies or research. It is based on the mystic, shadowy world of spirits, energy fields, and the supernatural. Psychic healing is based on ideas of health and disease that differ greatly from those of any other healing system.

The Most Ancient Healers

Psychic healing, still popular today, is the most ancient of all healing methods. Historians estimate that healers relied on spirits and the world of the supernatural one hundred thousand years ago. Tribes of prehistoric people relied on sacred healers, sometimes called *shamans,* for relief from pain and disease. Sacred healers worked in almost every area of the world, including Europe, Australia, Asia, and Africa. Ancient healers were also found among tribes of early Central, South, and North Americans.

Although the styles of healing differed among

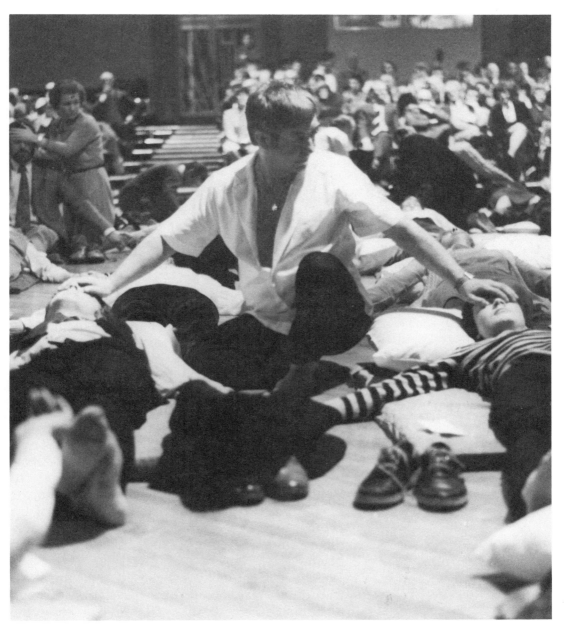

Psychic healers claim to be able to call on supernatural powers to heal people.

Left: This man is an African psychic healer. Right: This man is a Navajo healer. Both petition spirits from another world to help them.

various cultures, the basic ideas behind all ancient healing were the same. All these cultures believed that to be healthy, a person had to be in harmony with both his or her physical surroundings and *spiritual* surroundings. Spiritual could mean the person's relationship to the gods, or the feeling of being connected to all life, sometimes referred to as the *cosmic world*.

The psychic healers of prehistoric times believed that healing had to be done by means of a spiritual experience. As psychic researcher Alberto Villoldo states, the ill person had to "rediscover his connection to nature and to the divine. For this, the patient must step out of his ordinary state of awareness and into an extraordinary state where the journey back to health can begin."

The ancient healers believed that this "extraordinary state" could be achieved only through a shaman's help, for patients did not know the sacred healing art. Only shamans knew how to change their minds from an ordinary state to one allowing communication with the spirit world.

The methods for entering such a state varied among tribes. Some shamans used self-hypnosis; others used hallucinogenic herbs or plants to put themselves into the world of the spiritual. These plants made people hallucinate, or see things that did not really exist. Once shamans had entered the other world, they were able to do amazing things, people believed. They could use their minds to travel to different places. They could journey through time, for future, present, and past were distinctions that meant nothing to them. Most of all, shamans could communicate with the spirits of the great healers who had died. These healers shared vital information with the shamans that could make their patients well again.

Modern Psychic Healers

Today, few people live in tribes. The old idea of a shaman is almost nonexistent, although there are some who still practice their ancient healing arts in parts of North and South America, Australia, and the Philippine Islands.

Most of the shamans may be gone, but many of their ideas about health and disease live on. There are many kinds of psychic healers today, and though they differ in the specific methods of their healing arts, they all share a belief in the importance of the spiritual world.

Some modern psychic healers consult detailed astronomy maps, believing that the precise movements of stars and planets can guide them in their healing. Other healers study a patient's palms, or look intently at a patient's facial lines. Others depend on crystals or photographs taken with heat-sensitive equipment that indicate the amount of heat energy a patient's body gives off. Some feel that they can heal just by hearing a person's name—even though they may never have met the person!

Some psychic healers use hallucinogenic drugs (mushrooms, certain plant seeds, and other substances that cause the user to have visions) to help them contact the spirit world.

Psychic healers use many different methods to get in touch with powers that help them heal. Left: This woman uses a special deck of fortune-telling cards called Tarot. She uses it not only to tell a person's future, but to guide him or her to spiritual health. Right: Palmistry is another method used by psychic healers.

Besides approaching healing in different ways, modern psychic healers come from a wide variety of backgrounds. Some, particularly psychic healers in Western countries like the United States and England, heal by a mere touch, or even by concentrating positive thoughts toward their patients. Healers in South America or the Philippines are more aggressive about their cures. Many of these claim to be able to perform *psychic surgery,* the removal of tumors or diseased organs with their bare hands, using no surgical instruments.

Channeling Cosmic Energy

Many psychic healers are unable to explain exactly what it is they do. "I can look at a person and sometimes it's just as if I'm looking at the blueprints of a building," says psychic healer David Rathbone. "I see inside, and I just know where the structural weaknesses are. Sometimes when I walk into a crowded room, I immediately get a sense of who is sick—even if that person is not yet aware of it. I've even had the experience of

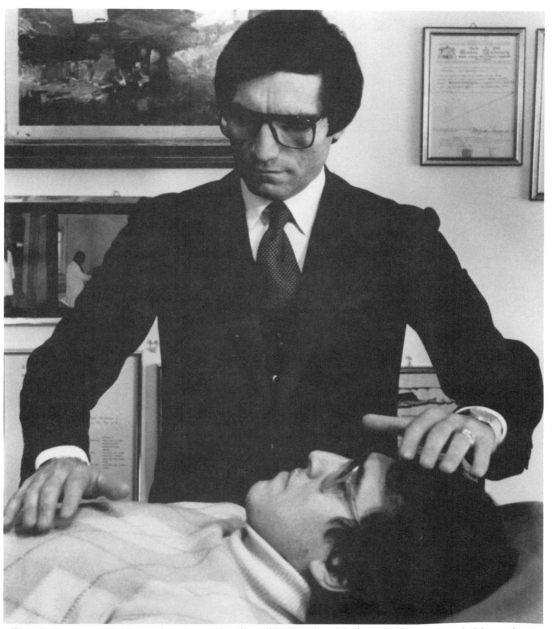

This Italian psychic is performing a healing. Notice that his hands do not touch his patient. Rather, he feels the energy fields around the person and works with that energy.

Harry Edwards was a famous English psychic who claimed to be able to heal even people who were at a great distance from him.

seeing Death, like a cloaked figure, standing near a person at an airport. I have no doubt that the person was terminally ill.''

Some psychics, like England's world-famous healer Harry Edwards, do not even need to see a person to be able to diagnose and treat the person's disease. Edwards, who died in 1976, found that he could heal people who were hundreds of miles away, merely by thinking about them. According to Edwards, he could accomplish this "absent healing," as he called it, more easily late at night than he could during the day. Although he was not sure of the reason, absent healing seemed to be more effective when everything was quiet and still.

Psychic researcher Paris Flammode interviewed Edwards, along with a number of other psychic healers. He found that most of them had some theories about why their healing method worked but admitted they were not certain. All agreed that their healing power was granted from a higher source, either God or some other

Valentine Greatrakes was an Irish psychic healer from the seventeenth century.

mystical being. Most felt, too, that they themselves were really not doing the healing.

Edwards saw his role as a channel—a go-between from the spiritual world to the physical world. There is, he believed, a huge source of energy throughout the universe. This energy surrounds the physical world and is made up of the feelings and powers of all who have ever lived. For while a physical body may age and die, the thoughts and energy of that body cannot disappear. These remain forever in the spiritual world.

A psychic healer, then, is one who can attune himself or herself to that world, so that its energy can be directed and used. Many healers believe that when they become attuned to the spiritual, they are helped by particular spirits. Sometimes referred to as "spirit guides" or "spirit intelligences," they assist the psychic in diagnosing and curing the patient.

Many of these spirit guides have supposedly revealed their names to their psychic healers. Many healers claim they are being assisted by the spirits of long-dead Zulus or Indian medicine men. Others, including Harry Edwards, claim that the spirits of such noted scientists as Louis Pasteur and Joseph Lister are their spiritual guides.

Patients who have been healed by psychics say that they have felt tingling, or a very warm feeling, in the diseased part of their body. Indeed, many healers say that when they place their hands on a patient, they, too, often feel a tingly sensation, much like an electric current, or else a heavy, hot feeling in their hands. Some psychics believe that this feeling is the transfer of energy from the spirit world to the patient.

The list of diseases that have been cured by these healers is impressive. According to Edwards and other healers like him, patients have been cured of cancer, diabetes, curvature of the spine,

"The weight of evidence today is massively in favor of spiritual healing."

Psychic healer Harry Edwards

"Because we are dealing here with desperate consumers with terminal illnesses who want to believe psychic surgery will cure them, no amount of disclosure will suffice to drive home to all the point that psychic surgery is nothing but a total hoax."

Federal Trade Commission, 1975

A psychic healing in Basel, Switzerland.

allergies, heart disease, and many other illnesses. Psychic healers also claim to have had great success with psychological diseases, such as paranoia and schizophrenia.

How many who visit psychic healers are cured? Many psychics guess that about half are helped. However, they are quick to point out that the majority of their patients have illnesses labeled "incurable" by the medical community. Harry Edwards, considered by many to be the greatest psychic healer of the twentieth century, estimated that about 35 percent of his patients were cured of their diseases.

Surgeon of the Rusty Knife

José Arigo died in an automobile crash in 1971. In the twenty years before his death, Arigo had become one of the most famous psychic healers in the world. His methods, dramatic and almost unbelievable in their success, were studied and filmed by many traditional doctors from the United States, Canada, and several European countries.

Arigo's methods differed dramatically from those of Edwards and other Western psychics. He not only diagnosed disease, he often "surgically" removed diseased tissue or malignant tumors. This surgery was done with no anesthetic or medical instruments. Arigo used any sharp object that was handy—a razor, an old pocketknife, or a scissor blade. This style of healing earned Arigo his nickname, "the surgeon of the rusty knife."

Arigo had almost no education; he was almost illiterate. He earned his living at a civil service job in the village of Congonhas de Campo in Brazil. He was a little overweight, and joked often about his gift of healing. He was a devout Catholic and believed strongly that half of people's medical problems were due to smoking and drinking.

In the evenings after his day job was over, Arigo would go to a little clinic in the town and heal the lines of people who waited for him. Arigo did his healing in a trance, and he did not remember anything about the healing when he was conscious. He had several spirit guides, the most important of whom was a German named Dr. Fritz. Fritz had died in World War I, exactly one year before Arigo was born.

While he was in his trance, Arigo relied on the diagnostic skills of his guide. Speaking to his patients in German (a language he did not know when conscious), Arigo would heal in a number of ways. After looking at a patient for a second or two, Arigo would nod his head and call out the disease or condition. Sometimes he would scribble out a prescription—in German, of course. Often the prescriptions called for drugs that either were very old and seldom used or else so new that the pharmacies in town had to order them from a larger city.

As mentioned earlier, Arigo did some surgery. An "operation" seldom lasted more than thirty seconds, and witnesses claim that there was little or no blood. One American doctor, Andrija Puharich, who visited Arigo with a team of

José Arigo was "the surgeon with a rusty knife," a psychic healer from Brazil. No one has ever been able to explain how he performed his miraculous cures.

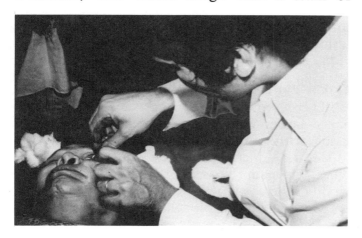

Ivan Trilha, a psychic healer from Paraguay, is shown performing psychic surgery on a woman's eye. If all goes as it is supposed to, the patient will feel no pain, will be cured when Trilha is finished, and will show no signs of the surgery he performed.

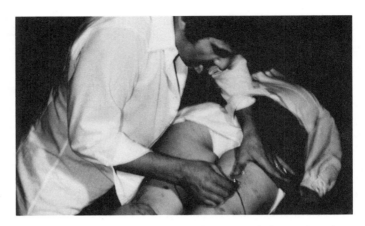

Left: José Mercado, a psychic surgeon from Granada. Right: Blood runs from the wounds of Ivan Trilha's patient. Yet when he is finished, there will be no scar.

researchers, was impressed. Puharich maintains that on more than one occasion he witnessed Arigo plunge a rusty knife behind the eyeball of a patient with cataracts. Using the knife blade, Arigo lifted the eyeball completely out of the socket and cut away the extra tissue. Throughout this procedure, the patient remained calm, even smiling.

Puharich saw Arigo do hundreds of healings in an evening, using the same blade on each. After an operation, Arigo would wipe the knife or scissors on his shirt, and go on to the next patient. It is estimated that Arigo attended to more than two million patients in the twenty years that he practiced psychic healing, curing many of them of serious diseases. He did not charge for his services.

Psychic Surgeons of the Philippines

There is another kind of psychic surgeon, this one a healer who removes diseased organs and tissues without making an incision. In Haiti, parts of Central America, and particularly the Philippines, there are many healers who practice a bloody type of surgery using their bare hands.

Most of the people who visit these surgeons are Americans who have given up hope of being cured by medical doctors. Many suffer from cancer, others from multiple sclerosis, blindness, cataracts, and other conditions. Many people have come back from their healing sessions claiming to be completely cured.

These psychic surgeons use similar methods. Like José Arigo, they avoid using anesthetic or worrying about the sterility of their surgical conditions. The operations frequently take place outdoors or in a back room of the healer's home.

After briefly examining the patient, the healer places his or her hands on the skin over the diseased area. An assistant stands ready, holding a bucket or basin. After kneading the skin, the surgeon's hands penetrate the patient's body. At this point there is a spurting fountain of blood, although patients claim afterwards that they felt no pain at all.

"To say I was a little apprehensive is an understatement," remembers Tanya Sabo, a 55-year-old woman from Dallas. She went to the Philippines with a group of thirty people, seeking a cure for a painful abdominal ailment.

"I had had no luck with doctors in Dallas—I must have seen twelve specialists over the last six years. When a friend of mine told me about someone she knew that had been cured of cancer—I said to myself, what do I have to lose?"

Sabo recalls how the healer told her that she would soon feel a warm, tingling sensation. "I heard a popping sound, and his hands were inside my stomach," she says. "There was a lot of blood, and I heard some of the people nearby gasp. After about thirty seconds, the healer pulled out several dark red blobs. He said they were blood clots, and that they were the cause of my problem.

"He threw the clots in the bucket and said that they were evil. He ordered his assistant to burn them. He splashed on something that looked like

"I cannot say I cured every case of cancer that has come to me, but cancer has been cured by spiritual healing."

Psychic healer Thomas Johanson

"That any intelligent person today could take psychic surgery seriously... is beyond belief."

Martin Gardner, The New Age

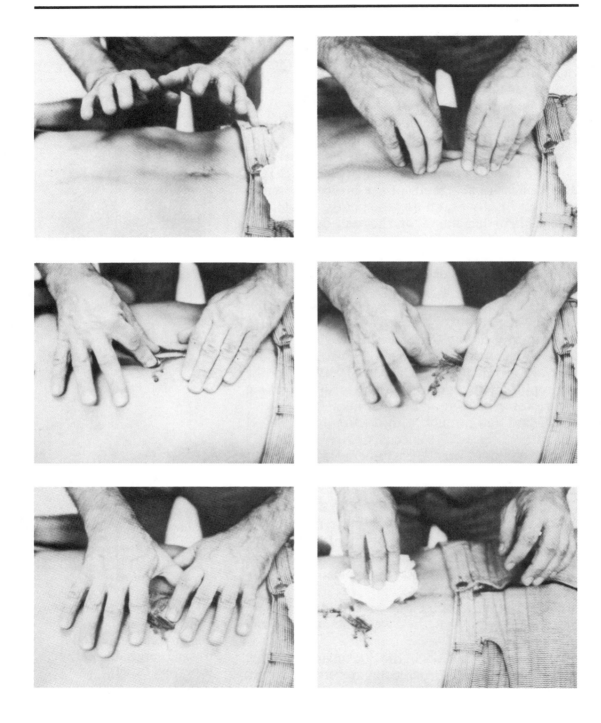

alcohol, and set fire to the bucket."

Sabo claims that when she stood up, only moments after her surgery, there was no trace of a scar, no trace that there had been any surgery at all. Best of all, she maintains, her abdominal pains disappeared. The psychic surgeon healed her, Sabo says, and she has recommended him to all of her friends with medical problems.

Criticism Abounds

Although there are hundreds—perhaps thousands—of people who feel they have been cured by psychic surgeons and healers, the medical community is highly critical. As psychic researcher John Taylor finds, "Hostility to [psychic] healers has always been shown by the medical profession. Supporting medical evidence both as to the nature of the disease being suffered and its subsequent progress is therefore scarce."

One problem, say critics, is that there do exist spontaneous cures for diseases as serious as cancer and advanced heart disease. A few patients who have been diagnosed as terminally ill, suddenly, for no apparent reason, become well. How can anyone know for sure whether it was a psychic who did the healing, or just an example of such a spontaneous cure? And what about the high percentage of diseases that result from stress and anxiety? If those negative emotions are relieved, if patients are reassured that they will get well, the symptoms usually disappear. Psychic healers provide that assurance, say critics. They give their patients hope, and those patients often respond by feeling better. But does that mean that cosmic energy or spiritual guides were the cause of the relief?

A Cruel Hoax?

Most Western psychic healers urge their patients to continue traditional medical care. They

Opposite: James Randi is a professional magician who believes psychic healers are frauds. He claims their "miraculous surgery" can be performed by anyone with a magician's skills. This series of pictures shows Randi's attempt at "psychic surgery." Top left: Randi places his hands on the "patient." Top right: Randi kneads and caresses the flesh, making a fold that resembles an incision. Middle left: Through Randi's sleight of hand, "blood" suddenly appears as he pretends to make an incision. Middle right: Randi removes tumor-like material from the "wound." Bottom left: The "incision" appears to close as the "tumor" is removed. Bottom right: Randi cleans the area up. No sign of surgery remains. Is Randi right? Is this how psychic surgeons perform their feats?

A psychic healer passes her hands over the patient. Many people claim to have been healed by such methods.

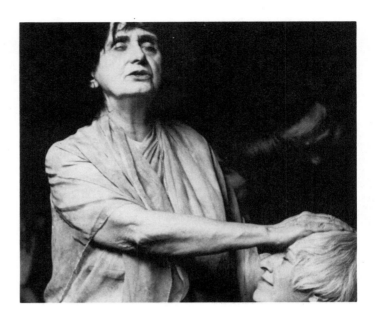

feel that their efforts are not a substitute for medical care, but rather that they can be effective in addition to that care.

This way of thinking is not the case, however, with psychic surgeons. People who submit to psychic surgery are led to believe that their diseases are cured when the clots or diseased tissues are removed from their bodies. It is for this reason that critics call psychic surgeons "dangerous."

Several researchers have investigated psychic surgeons and have described them as "hoaxes" or "quacks." Martin Gardner, in his book *The New Age,* describes the process of surgery without incision as nothing more than illusion. According to Gardner, this illusion is produced "by bending the fingertips so that the middle knuckles of the fingers press firmly on a patient's body. The tissues and blood, which usually come from animals, are concealed before the operation and produced at the appropriate time by the surgeon, who uses standard magician's sleight of hand to make them appear."

Other witnesses agree. Dr. William Nolen visited a psychic surgeon and himself went through an operation. He reported that the "clots" pulled from his abdomen were nothing more than pieces of cotton soaked in a red dye. Another investigator, who suspected that a "tumor" taken from a diseased patient was only animal tissue, was not allowed to inspect it. Instead, the surgeons demanded that it be burned immediately.

Another part of psychic surgery that makes it suspect to some authorities is the large amounts of money involved. One traditional doctor in the Philippines made inquiries about the fees of one psychic surgeon named Tony Agpaoa. Agpaoa saw at least three hundred patients each month and charged each one a minimum of two hundred dollars—a monthly income of over $60,000! Another psychic surgeon in Haiti admitted that his fee was four times higher for "rich Americans."

Although most authorities are certain that such healers are frauds, they are unsure about José Arigo of Brazil and his spiritual guide Dr. Fritz. Those critical of psychic healers usually put Arigo in another category, for his healing sessions were filmed and studied so carefully. No one has yet been able to understand how he was able to do the things he did.

"There are no failures in spiritual surgery, no matter what techniques are used."

Spiritual guide Dr. Fritz, quoted in *Healing States* by Alberto Villoldo

"Most psychic surgeons are sleight-of-hand artists who perform at night, by candlelight, with much distraction, in conditions that defy careful observation."

Dr. Andrew Weil, *Health and Healing*

Five

Can Natural Products Heal?

When a person is diagnosed as having cancer, traditional doctors may remove the diseased tissue or organ. They may follow this surgery with powerful doses of radiation or chemicals, designed to kill cancerous cells.

Many alternative healers disagree with such methods. They point out that the combination of surgery, chemicals, and radiation often leaves patients sicker and more uncomfortable than they should be. They point out, too, that cancer patients who have undergone such severe treatment often die because their bodies are too weak to fight off viruses or other infections.

Some alternatives promote less invasive remedies. They suggest that there are many disease-fighting substances found in nature—often in various foods or combinations of natural ingredients. And while many of these are believed to cure disease, others are used by healers to prevent problems from occurring.

Homeopathy

Homeopathy is an alternative healing system that dates back to the early nineteenth century. Samuel Hahnemann, a German physician, was

Opposite: This apothecary shop is filled with natural products that some people claim are the keys to health.

Samuel Hahnemann developed the practice called *homeopathy*. He used natural products—herbs and foods—to cure disease.

This man is cultivating cinchona trees, the plants that first inspired Hahnemann's philosophy of healing.

doing work on a substance called *cinchona*. Cinchona is a plant from which quinine, the remedy for malaria, comes.

Hahnemann did research in the typical fashion of a nineteenth-century scientist—he tried out the drug on himself. He was surprised to find that when he took cinchona, he developed symptoms of malaria such as chills and fever. Hahnemann, a healthy man, developed symptoms of malaria from the cure for malaria!

This discovery led Hahnemann to a new theory, that a substance that provokes disease symptoms in a healthy person can cure those same symptoms in a sick person if given in tiny amounts. Hahnemann experimented on other substances and became convinced that his theory was correct.

Coffee often has the effect of keeping people awake at night; Hahnemann found that tiny bits of coffee would cure sleeplessness. Many people allergic to bee stings develop life-threatening reactions. However, Hahnemann's experiments indicated that very small amounts of bee venom fend off such reactions. So convinced was he that his new form of healing was correct that in 1810 he published a book called *Organon of Healing.* The book lists many of his findings and the guidelines that he maintained were important in treating the sick.

Hahnemann found a great deal of pleasure in his discoveries, for they were a far different approach to healing than traditional medicine of the day. For many years he had been dissatisfied with what he termed the "inhumane measures" of physicians.

He lived in a time when antibiotics were yet unheard of, when the standard procedure for fighting illness was bleeding the patient. For this procedure, either lancets or leeches were used (see chapter 1). Drugs that were used often produced painful and severe side effects.

Homeopathy, as Hahnemann called his new brand of healing, seemed to him a good balance between gentle, humane care and the curing of disease. And because all of the more than two thousand substances Hahnemann worked with were found in nature (either animal, vegetable, or mineral), it seemed that homeopathy's remedies would work in harmony with the body's natural healing ability. This natural healing ability is the heart and soul of homeopathy.

How Does It Work?

It is important to remember that Hahnemann lived during a time when traditional medicine was not as respected an institution as it is today. There were no "proven" methods of healing, no detailed scientific studies, and people were often willing to try new ideas. And judging by the large number of deaths caused by aggressive doctors who bled their patients, it is quite probable that

"We know [homeopathy] works, but we just have not yet been able to explain why."

Dr. Elizabeth Hariveau, homeopathy researcher

"[Homeopathic] remedies are just placebos—no one has yet demonstrated their scientific validity."

Dr. William Jarvis, president, National Council Against Health Fraud

Unlike medical doctors, some homeopaths believe the symptoms of disease should not be suppressed. The symptoms, they believe, are signs that the body is fighting the disease itself.

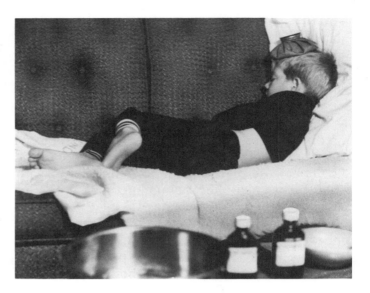

many people were more than anxious to believe in any gentler healing system!

Hahnemann called the body's natural healing instinct the "reactive system." Similar in many ways to what modern doctors call the immune system, the reactive system was responsible for fighting disease. Sometimes the body could be overwhelmed or confused with a disease, and therefore be unable to fight it effectively. A minute dose of a particular homeopathic substance—often so tiny as to be undetectable—could "prod" the reactive system so that it could fight back against disease and win.

Hahnemann believed, as do modern homeopaths, that traditional medicine is completely wrong when it comes to prescribing drugs. It is foolish, he thought, for doctors to concern themselves with repressing a patient's symptoms. Symptoms do not need to be managed or made to disappear. On the contrary, symptoms are evidence that the body is trying to rid itself of disease; they are not the disease itself.

For instance, if a child has a bad cold and runs

This Chinese drug company uses antlers, tiger bones, and numerous kinds of plant products in their production of homeopathic medicines.

a fever, homeopaths would not give aspirin or acetaminophen to suppress the fever. Instead, they would view the fever as the body's reactive system "kicking in." The presence of a fever would signal that the child's body was activating the white blood cells that would fight the cold. To suppress the fever would run the risk of suppressing the reactive system and lengthening the child's illness.

From the Royal Family to Mother Teresa

Today, millions of people worldwide believe in the healing powers of homeopathy, including such well-known people as Mother Teresa and Tina Turner. The royal family of Britain is reported to take along homeopathic kits when they travel. There are homeopathic clinics in the United States and in almost every country in Europe. Homeopathic remedies can be purchased in health food stores, many grocery stores, and drug stores.

One researcher found that in some European countries interest in homeopathy is booming. In France, for example, one third of all licensed physicians also practice homeopathy. And of the

Mother Teresa, the famous nun who cares for the poor of India, believes in homeopathy, as do millions of other people.

Homeopathic remedies are readily found in stores around the world.

20,000 pharmacies there, 90 percent carry a full selection of homeopathic remedies.

In the United States there are far fewer homeopathic healers. Researchers estimate that between 1,000 and 2,000 homeopaths practice in the U.S., and only about 300 of these are licensed physicians. However, many homeopathic remedies can be bought as easily in this country as in France or England, for their sale is not regulated by the government.

Stretching the Powers of Belief

There are several criticisms of homeopathy from the medical establishment. First and foremost, the lack of scientific data makes homeopathy suspect to traditional doctors. Believers in homeopathy admit that they aren't certain *why* it works, but they point out that scientists cannot explain why aspirin works, either.

There is a real problem in trying to prove that homeopathy works. To do so would require scientific testing, and that just is not possible, say homeopaths. Researchers would have to give homeopathic remedies to a large group of people and study the results. But one of the most important ideas of homeopathy is that each person has his or her own reactive system. Where traditional doctors diagnose a patient's disease by matching a list of common symptoms, the homeopath looks at the person as a whole. Eating habits, sleep patterns, whether one is a "morning person" or a "night person"—all are helpful to the homeopath in prescribing the proper treatment. As one researcher notes, "To give the same medication to many patients at one time, the obvious and only starting point for clinical research, is homeopathic heresy. Homeopaths insist on individualizing treatments."

Critics of homeopathy also find the idea of diluting remedies confusing. One of the main theories in Hahnemann's system is that the more a particular remedy is diluted, the more powerful it becomes. He called this "The Law of Infinitesimals." Some homeopathic medicines are diluted more than thirty times in water and alcohol solution. Many homeopathic substances have been diluted to 1 part in 100,000. Traditional doctors and researchers find it hard to believe that a lesser dose of a medicine would be longer-lasting and more powerful. As one medical researcher notes, "Science teaches us that the greater the number of molecules, the stronger a drug's effect. The Law of Infinitesimals stretches belief a little too far beyond the realm of good sense."

Paying Attention to Patients

How do critics explain the many claims of cures from homeopathic patients? For the most

"Extensive study of the relationship between cancer and food has shown that certain foods increase the incidence of malignancy, while others decrease the likelihood of ever developing the dreaded disease."

Dr. Albert Marchetti, pathologist

"Inspect any medical school textbook of medicine or ask your doctor. They will tell you that most diseases have nothing to do with diet."

Dr. Victor Herbert, Bronx VA Medical Center

A Native American medicine man purchases medicinal herbs. Some people believe it is the closeness between the healer and the patient that is the real "medicine."

part, they note that homeopaths spend a great deal of time listening to their patients. Because the method varies from one individual to another, healers must pay close attention to many aspects of a person's life—inner feelings, stress, and anxiety. Such close, concerned contact with their healer relieves many patients, say critics. And when patients are relieved of their anxieties, they generally get well faster. Homeopathic remedies tried on infants or animals (two groups that would probably not respond to such close questioning by a homeopath) have not been shown to be effective, critics point out.

Eating to Cure Disease

Almost any type of healer—traditional or alternative—would agree that certain foods are more healthful than others. We have been told about the major food groups—dairy, meat and fish, fruits and vegetables, and cereals—and that a certain amount from each is necessary each day. However, some alternative healing methods claim that certain foods are actually capable of curing serious diseases such as cancer.

Many popular alternative healing methods claim that the best way to fight a serious disease like cancer is through a *metabolic* approach. This means that, rather than treating the disease as a local one, healers should treat it as a condition of the entire body. Therefore, according to metabolic healers, a patient suffering from lung cancer will probably not get well from treatments concentrating on the lungs. The whole body, including all of the intricate systems of nerves, digestion, reproduction, and circulation, is interconnected. Cancer (and other diseases) is a breakdown in the stability of the whole person.

One of the first to voice this theory was Max Gerson, a German physician who died in 1959. As a young man he suffered from unbearably painful headaches. Traditional medicine was unable to help him find relief. Frustrated, Gerson began trying to cure himself.

He was a strong believer in the body's ability to heal itself of most things. Why, he wondered, were his migraine headaches such an impossible ailment for his own body to cure? Gerson's strongest suspicion was that his whole body was somehow out of balance. The reason, he theorized, could be the foods he was eating. If the

Many people believe that our food is contaminated by fertilizers and other pollutants. These chemicals keep us from remaining healthy. If we eat organically grown products, no chemicals added, our health will reap the benefits.

body were not getting enough of the correct foods, it would not be able to carry out its normal functions, such as healing itself.

The fact that many of the foods he ate were not completely pure bothered him. Gerson felt that because fertilizers were used in growing grains, fruits, and vegetables, and because many of the foods he ate were processed, he might be eating harmful substances. It would be far healthier, he decided, if he could limit his diet to nonprocessed, pure foods.

He began by drinking only milk, theorizing that because it was a baby's first food, it must be the healthiest. However, his headaches became more frequent and more severe. Perhaps, thought Gerson, milk is *not* healthy for humans once they reach adulthood.

He turned to fresh fruits, vegetables, and grains. He ate no meat, for he strongly believed that the human digestive tract was, by its design, not well equipped to chemically break down meat. Gerson found that on this diet his headaches disappeared. Over the next several years, Gerson offered his diet to his patients who also suffered from migraine headaches. The results were as positive for them as for Gerson himself.

Not Just for Headaches

One of his patients mentioned that not only had her headaches disappeared after beginning the diet, but the skin disease caused by her severe tuberculosis disappeared as well. This finding led to more experiments with patients suffering from that disease, most of them terminally ill. Eliminating everything except fresh fruits, vegetables, and grains cured the skin tuberculosis as completely as it had the migraines. In one famous experiment, 450 patients suffering from terminal skin tuberculosis were placed on Gerson's diet, and 447 of them recovered.

Opposite: Max Gerson developed a metabolic approach to health. That is, by eating the proper foods—mostly organically grown grains, fruits, and vegetables—the body's health system will stay in balance and the person will stay well.

Helene Schweitzer used Gerson's eating plan to regain her health.

Over the years Gerson found that his diet cured many conditions that were often incurable by traditional medical methods. One of his most famous patients was Helene Schweitzer, wife of Dr. Albert Schweitzer. She had become deathly ill with lung tuberculosis. Gerson's diet enabled her to make a complete and full recovery. Schweitzer, a famous doctor and founder of a hospital in Africa, became a believer in Gerson's diet.

At the core of the Gerson therapy, as it is now called, is the idea that most serious diseases are caused by an imbalance in the body. Chemical impurities, poisons, and additives have replaced most of the nutrients in our food. However, when the body is stabilized with pure, wholesome, nutritious food, it can repair itself—even when disease has already struck.

In the case of cancer, which is the main focus of the Gerson therapy today, the location or size of the malignant tumor is not the most important thing, according to Gerson. "What is essential,"

Gerson writes, "is not the growth itself or the visible symptoms; it is the damage of the whole metabolism, including the loss of defense, immunity, and healing power." By maintaining the diet, the body can regain its defenses.

Promising Results

Like other metabolic healing alternatives, Gerson's therapy relies on strict adherence to the diet. Patients who decide to give Gerson's therapy a try visit his clinic on the west coast of Mexico. The clinic, run by Gerson's daughter Charlotte, closely monitors each patient's food and beverage intake.

Most of the food consists of fresh fruits and vegetables. None are frozen, canned, or processed in any way. All have been grown organically—without pesticides or chemical fertilizers.

Each patient drinks thirteen glasses of juice made from vegetables and fruits per day. In addition, powerful doses of vitamins and minerals are given, as well as three glasses of fresh baby calf's liver juice, which is high in nutrients. Enemas

A woman picks out food to keep her healthy.

Traditional medical doctors do not believe that simply eating the right foods can prevent or cure such severe diseases as cancer. Doctors are concerned that patients who religiously follow a natural products philosophy will fail to obtain needed medical treatment.

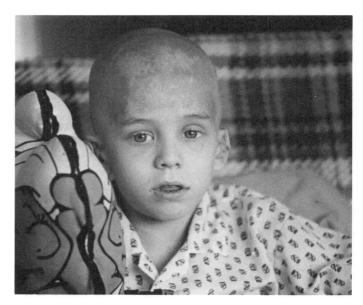

made of coffee are injected into the intestines to clean out the lower part of the digestive tract. Gerson's therapy requires the removal of all traces of poison and impurities from the body.

Gerson's clinic claims to be very successful in curing the cancer patients they have been seeing over the past thirty years. Gerson's staff boast that they have either cured or drastically improved half of the patients that had been diagnosed as terminally ill by the medical establishment. Even more dramatic, they say that the diet totally eliminates the patient's pain within a day or two.

Objections from Doctors

As long as Gerson's therapy and other metabolic cancer therapies have been claiming to heal people, traditional doctors have criticized these methods. One strong objection is that people will try a "painless" diet rather than submit to surgery, radiation, or chemotherapy—the standard means of fighting cancer. Gerson's staff has said that they prefer that patients not come to them weakened by the highly toxic chemotherapy. "In cancer therapy," said Dr. Curtis Hesse, former director of the clinic, "we do not as a general rule accept any patient who has undergone chemotherapy. From past experience, we know that liver damage and damage to other organs, as well as the immune system, have been such that they do well for a two- to three week period but then go downhill."

Traditional doctors are concerned that reliance on diet alone will waste valuable time. "I'm greatly distressed that a patient might remove himself from proven, traditional treatment—or not seek it at all. When the diet fails, and the patient realizes his mistake, it might be too late for proven cancer treatment to be effective," states Dr. Herman Wilken, a critic of the metabolic approach.

The "provability" of such cancer remedies worries others, too. In 1988 the National Cancer Institute published a paper critical of Gerson's therapy. The NCI claims that it has reviewed ten of Gerson's cases and has found "no convincing evidence that this treatment worked, particularly since the patients were also receiving other anticancer treatments." In other words, since the ten patients whose cancers disappeared were also using some traditional medical healing, there was no scientific proof that Gerson's metabolic therapy is what cured them.

As for other diets and vitamin regimens, the Institute remains skeptical. "We have no evidence at this time that cancer can be treated successfully with special diets or dietary elements or that the disease recurrence can be prevented through diet." Until scientific proof can be offered to the contrary, this remains the official position of traditional medicine.

"Traditional cancer therapy...is not very successful at eradicating symptoms and fails abysmally at preventing recurrences."

Gary Null, *Gary Null's Complete Guide to Healing Your Body Naturally*

"Quackery and food fads become dangerous, unmitigated evils when their false promises keep people from seeking medical treatment that might have saved their lives."

Dr. Hilde Bruche, Baylor College of Medicine

Six

Can Touch Heal?

Spiritual and psychic healers say they frequently use touch to transfer healing power from the spirit world to their patients. Faith healers believe that by touching someone they can call forth God's healing power and cure disease. But the use of touch in healing is not limited to spiritual or faith healers. Some alternatives to traditional medicine claim that touching and massaging can be valuable tools in curing and diagnosing disease. Such healing methods are not based on any religious or spiritual belief, either by the healer or the patient.

Designed for Touching

Those who stress touch as a healing method point to the worldwide use of touch to calm and console. A rub, a hug, a pat, a caress—all are used as an unspoken way of reassuring someone who is nervous or upset. This is the basis of touch healing, although its advocates say that touch can do far more.

The human body is constructed in such a way that touch is its most basic sense, say touch healers. The eighteen square feet of skin on the average person is dotted with millions of tiny touch receptors. Every square inch of human skin also contains fifteen feet of blood vessels and over seventy feet of nerves. When touched—even

Can illness be cured by touch? Many people believe the human organism is designed to be responsive to it.

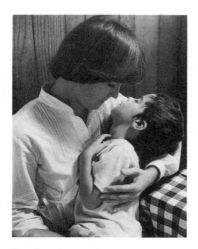

Studies have shown that even extremely sick people and animals respond to a loving touch.

lightly—this network of nerves and receptors is set into motion.

So important and basic is the sense of touch that some scientists claim that the skin is even more important than the brain. They point to a little boy named Benjamin, born without a brain. He has a brain stem, the rudimentary part of the brain that handles such activities as breathing and heartbeat. Benjamin is unable to see, taste, hear, smell, or think even the simplest thought. Yet he can feel. When his nurses pick him up and fondle him, the little boy reacts by smiling and laughing. Only touch connects Benjamin to the world.

Changing Attitudes Toward Touching

Because it is so basic, one might assume that touch has always been encouraged by the medical establishment. That is not so. Less than one hundred years ago, doctors and nurses in the United States were discouraged from touching patients. They were told by scientists that touch was dangerous, for it spread germs and disease.

One striking example of this occurred in the early 1900s in hospital orphanages for infants, called foundling homes. Foundling homes existed in almost every large town and city in America. Well-trained staffs with the most up-to-date equipment cared for the many babies who were brought to the homes.

Day after day, month after month, the babies lay in their clean little beds. They were not held during feedings; instead, little platforms called bottle props were used to position the bottle to each baby's mouth. Every precaution was taken to make sure the babies were kept germfree.

However, almost all the babies at these foundling homes died! As late as 1924, the death rate for infants in these clean, modern hospitals was close to 100 percent.

Babies who are not picked up sometimes succumb to a "failure to thrive" syndrome. In the early twentieth century, orphanages changed their policies so that children would be held and played with by those who cared for them. This simple change reduced the death rate at such institutions.

An American doctor who visited Germany observed conditions in a foundling home there. He noticed that a heavy old woman would sometimes shuffle into the area where the sickest babies were kept. Without gloves or surgical mask, the woman would pick up a baby and sit with it in a rocking chair. Hour after hour the woman would cuddle, stroke, and sing to the baby.

When the doctor asked his guides about the woman, he was told that she cared for the babies who seemed to be near death. When the staff was sure that their medicines were not going to work, they let "Old Anna," as she was known, hold the babies. And surprisingly, many of those babies got well!

The American doctor took this information home and began a new policy in foundling homes. From that time forward, nurses were encouraged to touch the babies. And babies who had once been listless, with grayish skin and faint heartbeats, began to thrive. Over the next fifteen years, the death rate in foundling homes dropped to less than 10 percent.

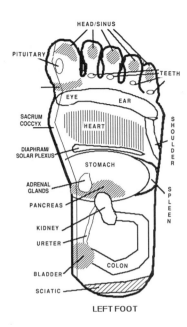

HEAD/SINUS

PITUITARY

TEETH

EYE

EAR

SACRUM
COCCYX

HEART

SHOULDER

DIAPHRAM/
SOLAR PLEXUS

STOMACH

ADRENAL
GLANDS

SPLEEN

PANCREAS

KIDNEY

URETER

COLON

BLADDER

SCIATIC

LEFT FOOT

Touch therapists use touch both for overall well-being and to remedy specific complaints. Right: A therapist uses touch on a patient's foot. Left: A diagram of the places on the left foot that correspond to areas of the body.

Ch'i: The Vital Energy Force

Touching as an alternative form of healing uses such examples to show the powerful need humans have to be touched. That touching can be the difference between life and death to humans and other animals has been documented by several scientific researchers over the past fifty years. But the roots of touch healing go back even farther.

The basis of several touch healing methods is Chinese medicine. According to medical principles developed more than four thousand years ago, every human has an energy flow, called a *ch'i*. The ch'i is what keeps the body and mind in the correct balance. When the ch'i is functioning properly, the person experiences health and peace of mind. When something interferes with the energy flow—poor diet, stress, and so on—bad health is the result.

The ancient Chinese believed that the body has various meridians, or channels, through which the ch'i flows. There are hundreds of points along these meridians where the ch'i can be stimulated back into balance. If the flow of the ch'i was interrupted, or if it was obstructed along the meridians, a healer could change the ch'i. This change could occur by applying pressure or even by puncturing these points. Today's well-known practices of acupressure and acupuncture are based on these basic ideas.

Ancient Roots, Modern Methods

The Chinese believe that the idea for acupressure and acupuncture was a result of an ancient battle. An emperor's warriors had been ambushed by enemies, the story goes. Many of the warriors reported to the emperor that, although they had been hit time and again with sharp spears, their pain had often disappeared. Not only that, but as long as the spear points and arrowheads remained in their bodies, many of their chronic illnesses disappeared. The warriors reported relief from asthma, depression, headaches, and other health problems.

Over time, the Chinese experimented with the idea of applying firm pressure with the hands on key points along the body's meridians. Besides pressure, they used needles to puncture these key points, hoping to stimulate the flow of healing energy.

Over the centuries, scholars mapped out the various points on the body's skin surface that were responsive to pressure and puncture. They drew intricate diagrams showing the connection between these points on the skin and the health of various body organs. It was interesting to them that the key points for healing certain injuries or illnesses usually were nowhere near the site of the problem! By puncturing the skin near the ankle, for instance, they might bring relief to a woman suffering from a sore neck. Applying pressure to a man's ear might help the arthritis in his shoulder.

Modern Acupuncture

Although most of the principles of acu-

"I came in here with pain in my back. I leave with no pain. I don't care how it works. It works—period!"

Owen Landis, acupuncture patient

"[Acupuncture's] premise involves history and assumptions that are alien to Western culture; one cannot read about meridians or energy in a Harvard Medical School textbook."

Sherry Suib Cohen, *The Magic of Touch*

Right: The Shiatsu practitioner (a kind of touch therapist) is careful to exert pressure at exactly the right locations to do the patient the most good. Opposite page: Over the past several centuries, detailed charts have evolved that show sensitive points on the body. These points relate to specific kinds of problems. They respond to acupressure and acupuncture.

pressure and acupuncture have not changed, some of the methods have been modernized. Most of the changes have occurred in the type of equipment used. The first acupuncture needles were made of finely polished stone, bone fragments, or bamboo. Over the centuries, Chinese surgeons learned to fashion them out of gold and silver. Today's needles are usually made of stainless steel. They are more slender than their ancient counterparts. Machines today can make needles almost as fine as a human hair—less than 1/17,000th of an inch thick!

After diagnosing a patient's problem, the acupuncturist determines the best placement of needles. The needles may be left in for a few seconds or a few hours. The length of time and depth of the needles depends on the severity and type of health problem.

Acupuncturists today frequently twirl needles for extra stimulation to the ch'i. Often, too, they attach faint electrical currents to the needles. Patients say there is no pain, either from the insertion of the needles or from the electrical current.

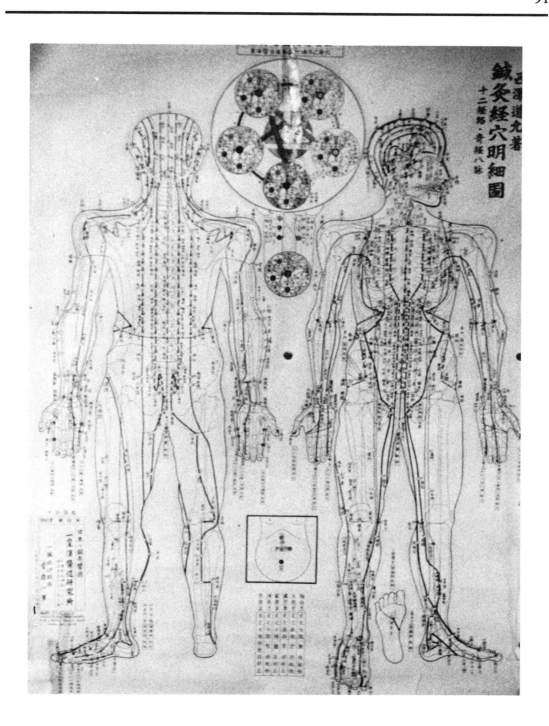

Chinese students studying acupuncture.

They report a tingling feeling, usually followed by a relief from any pain they had been suffering.

Growing Interest

Although acupressure and acupuncture are most common in China and other Oriental countries, they are becoming established in other places. Acupuncture is used in hospitals in Germany, France, Sweden, and the Soviet Union. In the United States more than 12,000 doctors use acupuncture either in surgery or pain therapy.

"I am aware that many of my patients are skeptical," says one Chicago doctor. "I have been using acupuncture as a tool for about nine years. I've found it to be a valuable help in keeping my arthritis patients' chronic pain to a minimum. I have also used it in surgery as an alternative to chemical anesthetic.

"The usual reaction from my patients is 'Oh, no—you're not going to stick needles in me!' I know lots of people are scared to death of needles. But they soon see that these are not like hypodermic needles, or sewing needles, or

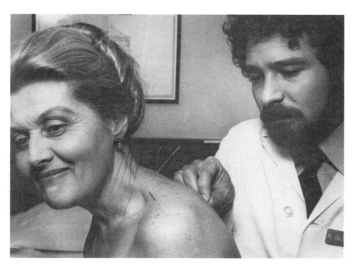 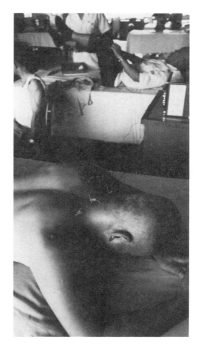

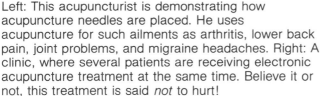

Left: This acupuncturist is demonstrating how acupuncture needles are placed. He uses acupuncture for such ailments as arthritis, lower back pain, joint problems, and migraine headaches. Right: A clinic, where several patients are receiving electronic acupuncture treatment at the same time. Believe it or not, this treatment is said *not* to hurt!

whatever they are expecting. I've never had anyone complain of pain or discomfort from acupuncture treatment."

Does It Really Work?

Millions of doctors and patients around the world feel that acupuncture is a valuable healing method. Although in the United States acupuncture is used mainly as an anesthetic or for control of chronic pain, its advocates claim it can treat a large number of ailments. High blood pressure, ulcers, asthma, bronchitis, migraine headaches, skin diseases, and depression have been successfully treated with acupuncture. Many doctors are using it to help chemically dependent people break their addiction. Others are using it to help people with eating disorders like obesity and anorexia nervosa.

But many in the medical establishment are less enthusiastic. Some hesitate to support a healing method based on energy flows and meridians. These terms are not found in standard medical textbooks, at least in the United States. Ch'i is a concept that cannot be proved, measured, or tested in a way satisfactory to many scientists.

Other matters concern medical doctors, too. Some worry about the danger of improperly placed needles. They point to instances where patients have had collapsed lungs from acupuncture needles. There are other reports of puncture of the kidneys, bladder, and the uterus of a pregnant woman.

Finally, some doctors worry that because acupuncture is a healing alternative, it is not subject to the same rigorous standards as traditional medicine. They are concerned that acupuncture needles might be used on more than one person, thereby risking the spread of diseases such as hepatitis or AIDS.

These illustrations show some of the things a touch therapist must learn. Left: The therapist "scans" the patient's head to try to perceive changes in temperature. Middle: The therapist runs her hands down the patient's body, without actually touching it, searching for signs of congestion or imbalance. The therapist might feel heat, cold, tingling, pressure, slight electric shocks, or pulsations. Right: The therapist "unruffles" congested areas before directing energy to particular parts of the body for healing purposes.

Therapeutic Touch—Another Healing Alternative

Several healing alternatives are based on the Chinese ideas of meridians and ch'i. One that has grown enormously in popularity in the United States is called "therapeutic touch." Its chief advocate is Dolores Krieger, a retired professor of nursing at New York University.

Krieger first became interested in the idea in 1968 when she studied firsthand a Hungarian healer named Oskar Estabany. Estabany had had a great deal of success in healing animals and people by placing his hands upon them and concentrating. Krieger was convinced that Estabany's healing was real; she also believed that it was possible for touch healing to be taught to others. Over the next several years she did just that, developing a technique that could be easily taught and easily learned. Since her technique was developed, Krieger and her associates have taught more than 15,000 people therapeutic touch.

Some of what she bases her method on is the Chinese philosophy of energy fields. Krieger believes that many health problems, such as depression, fever, infection, and inflammation, are caused by imbalances in a person's flow of energy. The job of a healer is not to "perform miracles" by the laying on of hands. Rather, it is to assist a patient's body to heal itself.

The method she teaches has five steps. The first is called "centering." It is important that there is nothing in the healer's mind but the patient. All outside distractions, such as bright lights and loud noise, must be screened out.

The second step, called "assessment," requires a great deal of sensitivity on the part of the healer. She must run her hands along the patient's body, locating any areas that feel out of balance. Surprisingly, the healer rarely touches the skin of the patient. Instead, she jerkily moves her hands

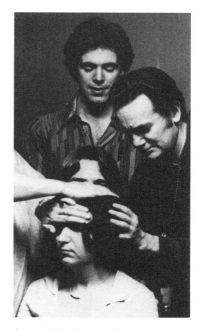

A psychic therapist at work. Doctors, patients, and therapists debate whether such methods actually work.

about two inches above the patient's body. Though this often takes months of training, it is possible to detect imbalances. To the healer, these areas may generate heat or coolness or a prickling feeling.

The third step in therapeutic touch is to unruffle the energy field—to sweep or brush the energy, improving the flow of the energy to all injured or diseased areas. After this, the healer normalizes the energy flow. This, claims Krieger, involves a transfer of thought from the mind of the healer to the patient. For instance, if the healer detects areas of heat in a patient, she may think of cool colors or other images to lessen the heat.

The fifth step is, simply, knowing when it is time to stop. Sometimes, says Krieger, a patient's energy flow can become overloaded by too much manipulation. It is then best to quit and try again later.

The Effectiveness of Therapeutic Touch

Krieger claims that more than 95 percent of the patients who undergo therapeutic touch experience relaxation. She also notes that there is almost always a relief from pain. She realizes that many of her colleagues in the medical establishment require tests and studies to prove such claims, and she feels that her healing method has stood up to such testing.

In one test done between 1971 and 1975, Krieger did a study of the red blood cells of patients. She monitored the amount of oxygen (important for healing) in each cell. She found that those patients who had undergone therapeutic touch had more oxygen in their blood than patients who had not been touched.

Another test was done by Dr. Janet Quinn at the University of South Carolina. She wanted to find out whether therapeutic touch really reduced patients' anxiety levels. In her tests, she found that anxiety was indeed reduced, even among those who were not aware that they were being "healed" by touch!

Many Doubts

Like acupuncture and acupressure, this type of touch therapy has many skeptics. Energy fields that can be "swept away" or changed by the thought patterns of a healer are not considered scientific, at least in the United States. Even those who acknowledge the existence of individual fields of energy or electricity around humans say that such fields are too small to be affected by another person.

Some scientists have criticized Krieger's research. They say that Krieger did not do adequate tests of blood oxygen before the therapeutic touch was done; therefore it would be difficult to credit the healing method for the increase in oxygen.

Scientists have criticized the anxiety-reducing success, too. Krieger had a trained interviewer conduct a question-and-answer session on how individual patients felt after their touch session. A more accurate measurement, say some scientists, would be pulse, blood pressure, and skin tests which could show the degree of anxiety.

"Krieger frequently and explicitly states that her method is not miraculous. But it most certainly is. In fact, therapeutic touch is a modern-day classic of a miracle."

Clinical psychologist Jules Older, *Touching Is Healing*

"If a patient feels more relaxed after a session of therapeutic touch, is it because [the energy field] has been unruffled or because the healer's voice and manner were soothing?"

Dr. Paul Reisser, co-author of *New Age Medicine*

Conclusion

The Search For Answers Continues

Do alternative methods of healing work? Millions of people claim they do, although proving that to the scientific community has been a problem. Whether such healing methods as natural healing, homeopathy, faith healing, psychic surgery, iridology, and others will become accepted by traditional doctors in the future remains a mystery.

Some researchers like to speculate on what medicine will be like in the twenty-first century. Certainly there will be new wonder drugs and exciting new technology that will enable doctors to treat and diagnose diseases much earlier. But there is reason, too, to expect that at least some alternative healing methods will be used. After all, a recent Harris poll showed that only 35 percent of Americans were "very satisfied" with the traditional health care they received during the year 1988. With such a large number of dissatisfied customers, it seems reasonable to guess that many people will try other methods of healing.

Some futurists feel that the medicine of the twenty-first century will be forced to change according to changing health needs. More and more people will be ill with diseases such as AIDS that

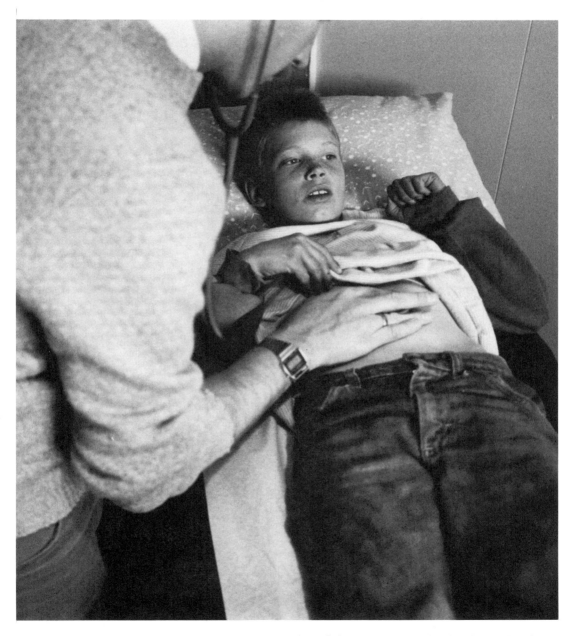

What will the future bring in the field of medicine? Some think the family doctor is still the best health practitioner for most people.

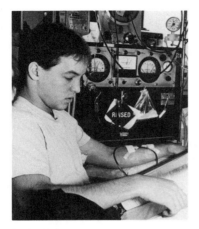

Left: A young man on a dialysis machine, a high-tech treatment that does the work for his inadequate kidney. Right: A psychic healer's waiting room. Some experts think medicine of the future will combine medical technology and alternative healing methods to bring the best health care to more people.

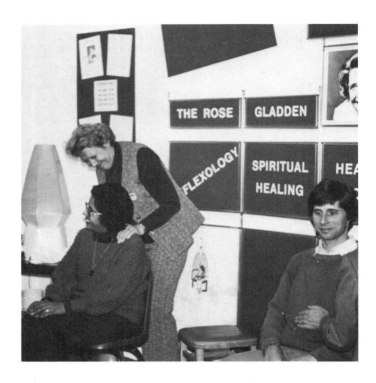

have no known cure. Many health care professionals grimly predict that such diseases will reach epidemic proportions, with traditional medicine unable to cure them.

More common, too, will be viruses that are untreatable with modern drugs or remedies. And because doctors are prescribing such large amounts of antibiotics, many diseases that were formerly treatable will build up resistance to penicillin and other medicines. This will certainly change the way doctors of the future can do their healing.

Some researchers speculate that tomorrow's healers will be more humane and more personal. Doctors of tomorrow may borrow certain elements from some alternative healing methods. They may find that they are more successful when they look at the spiritual, psychological, and physical sides of each patient. Since so many diseases are caused by the daily stresses and anxieties of life, doctors' diagnoses may be more accurate because they really know their patients.

One Chicago internist admits that she is unsure about the direction medicine will take. "I don't know how much of these [alternative] methods I buy into—or whether I buy into any," she says. "But I will bet my last dollar that the best doctors of tomorrow will be the ones with the open minds. They're the ones who will be moving forward, while the rest of us are standing still."

Bibliography

David Alexander, "A Closer Look at Today's Faith Healers," *The Humanist*, Sept.-Oct. 1988.

Lila L. Anastas, *How to Stay Out of the Hospital*. Emmaus, PA: Rodale, 1986.

Margery Blackie, *The Patient, Not the Cure*. Santa Barbara, CA: Woodbridge, 1978.

Mary Carpenter, "Homeopathic Chic," *Health*, March 1989.

Matt Clark, "A Strange Sort of Therapy," *Newsweek*, Oct. 20, 1974.

Norman Cousins, "The Mind as Apothecary," *Consumers Digest*, March-April 1985.

Ronald Deutsch, *The New Nuts Among the Berries*. Palo Alto, CA: Bull, 1986.

Mark Donald, "The Natural," *Gentlemen's Quarterly*, May 1989.

"Faith, Hands and Auras," *Time*, October 16, 1972.

Paris Flammonde, *The Mystic Healers*. New York: Stein and Day, 1974.

John G. Fuller, *Arigo: Surgeon of the Rusty Knife*. New York: Thomas Y. Crowell, 1974.

Winifred Gallagher, "The Healing Touch," *American Health*, October, 1988.

Martin Gardner, *The New Age*. Buffalo, NY: Prometheus, 1988.

Norman Gevitz (ed.), *Other Healers*. Baltimore: Johns Hopkins, 1988.

Marcia Gillespie, "Healer Meyerson," *Ms.*, December, 1985.

Richard Grossinger, *Planet Medicine*. Garden City, NY: Anchor, 1980.

Michael Harner, *The Way of the Shaman*. San Francisco: Harper and Row, 1980.

Victor Herbert, *Nutritional Cultism*. Philadelphia: George F. Stickley Co., 1980.

John Leo, "One Laugh = 3 Tbsp. Oat Bran," *US News & World Report*, January 23, 1989.

Steven Locke and Douglas Colligan, "Mind Cures," *Omni*, March 1986.

Meredith McGuire, *Ritual Healing in Suburban America*. New Brunswick: Rutgers, 1988.

Albert Marchetti, *Beating the Odds*. Chicago: Contemporary Books, 1988.

Simon Mills, *Alternatives in Healing*. New York: New American Library, 1988.

"Mind Over Cancer," *Prevention,* March 1988.

Raymond A. Moody, *Laugh After Laugh*. Jacksonville, FL: Headwaters, 1978.

Michael Moore and Lynda J. Moore, *The Complete Handbook of Holistic Health*. Englewood Cliffs, NJ: Prentice-Hall, 1983.

William A. Nolen, *Healing*. New York: Random House, 1974.

Gary Null, *Gary Null's Complete Guide to Healing Your Body Naturally*. New York: McGraw Hill, 1988.

Jules Older, *Touching Is Healing*. New York: Stein and Day, 1982.

James Randi, *The Faith Healers*. Buffalo, NY: Prometheus, 1989.

Paul Reisser, Teri K. Reisser, and John Weldon, *New Age Medicine*. Chattanooga, TN: Global, 1988.

Douglas Stalker (ed.), *Examining Holistic Medicine*. Buffalo, NY: Prometheus, 1985.

Jess Stearn, *The Miracle Workers*. Garden City, NY: Doubleday, 1972.

John Taylor, *Science and the Supernatural*. New York: Dutton, 1980.

Dana Ullman, "Homeopathy: Medicine for the 21st Century," *The Futurist*, July-Aug. 1988.

Alberto Villoldo, *Healing States*. New York: Simon and Schuster, 1986.

Roy Wallis (ed.), *Marginal Medicine*. New York: Macmillan, 1976.

Andrew Weil, *Health and Healing*. New York: Houghton Mifflin, 1983.

Ann Weiss, *Biofeedback*. New York: Franklin Watts, 1984.

James H. Young, *The Medical Messiahs*. Princeton, NJ: Princeton University Press, 1967.

Index

Picture Credits

AP/Wide World, 11, 18, 34T, 34B, 41, 46, 49, 54R, 56L, 70B, 72, 74, 78, 80, 82, 86, 100L

Magnum Photos: Erich Hartmann 12; David Hurn 21; Steve McCurry 28, 31, 32; Burt Glinn 33; Paul Fusco 45L, 45R, 47, 88R; Eve Arnold 73T; Leonard Freed 85; Elliott Erwitt 90, 91; Eli Reed 99

©Ira Block, 14, 69, 76, 77, 81

National University of Medicine, 16T

Mary Evans Picture Library, 16B, 17, 24, 25, 26, 29, 53, 58T, 58B, 60, 100R

Bettmann Archive, 22, 30, 43, 70T, 73B, 87, 92, 93L

Stock Boston: Jeffry W. Myers 37; Ira Kirschenbaum 38; Jeff Albertson 44; Jack Prelutsky 56R; Peter Simon 66, 95

Amy Johnson, 39, 88L, 94

Robert Waltman, photographer, Aims Community College, Greeley, CO, 50

©Nathan Benn/Woodfin Camp, Inc., (1983) 54L, (1982) 55, 93R

Fortean Picture Library/Dr. Elmar R. Gruber, 57, 61B, 62R

Photographs from *Arigo: Surgeon of the Rusty Knife* by John G. Fuller; copyright ©1974 by John G. Fuller, reprinted by permission of Harper & Row, Publishers, Inc., 61T

Technology Review, 62L, 64

About the Author

Gail Stewart received her undergraduate degree from Gustavus Adolphus College in St. Peter, Minnesota. She did her graduate work in English, linguistics, and curriculum study at the College of St. Thomas and the University of Minnesota. Gail taught English and reading for more than ten years.

She has written forty-five books for young people, including a six-part series called *Living Spaces*. This is her second Great Mysteries book.

Gail and her husband live in Minneapolis with their three sons, two dogs, and a cat. She enjoys reading (especially children's books) and playing tennis.